W9-CYZ-088

CHAPLIN

CHAPLIN

The Mirror of Opinion

DAVID ROBINSON

5 79847

Secker & Warburg
London

Indiana University Press
Bloomington

First published in England 1983 by
Martin Secker & Warburg Limited
54 Poland Street, London W1V 3DF
and in the United States by
Indiana University Press
Tenth and Morton Streets
Bloomington, Indiana

British Library Cataloguing in Publication Data
Robinson, David, *1930–*
    Chaplin.
    1. Chaplin Charles, *1889–1977*   2. Moving-picture
    actors and actresses—United States—Biography
    I. Title
    791.43′028′0924   PN2287.C5
ISBN 0–436–42053–8
ISBN 0–436–42052–X (Pbk.)

Library of Congress Cataloging in Publication Data
Robinson, David, 1930–
    Chaplin, the mirror of opinion.
    Filmography: p.
    1. Chaplin, Charlie, 1889–1977.   2. Moving-picture
actors and actresses—United States—Biography.
3. Comedians—United States—Biography.   I. Title.
PN2287.C5R57   1983   791.43′028′0924   [B]   82–48615
ISBN 0–253–11178–1
ISBN 0–253–21160–3 (pbk.)

Filmset in Monophoto Times by
Northumberland Press Ltd, Gateshead
Printed in Great Britain by
Richard Clay (The Chaucer Press) Ltd,
Bungay, Suffolk

Contents

Introduction

'About Chaplin,' wrote Gilbert Seldes a world ago, in 1937, 'everything has been written, everything true and false, everything silly and wise, everything romantic and critical, and the same things will continue to be written for a long time to come.' When a Swedish bibliographer, Lennart Eriksson, compiled a list of books on Chaplin in 1980 he found well over five hundred titles, in thirty-seven languages from Hindi to Yiddish, Azerbaijani to Javanese. Few of them have added anything to the basic facts of Theodore Huff's 1951 biography and Chaplin's own story, *My Autobiography*, published in 1964.

One day, perhaps, there will be more details to add to the record. Papers of Edna Purviance and Fred Karno are known to exist in private collections, but still remain inaccessible to researchers. Chaplin's own documents are still closely guarded and seem likely to remain so. John McCabe recalls that he approached his own *Charlie Chaplin*, which must now be regarded as a standard biography, with much misgiving: 'Surely no man in film history has been more written about, more documented. It must all have been done'.

Since McCabe, the misgivings and reluctance to attempt a new book on Chaplin are only the greater. No doubt all intending writers on Chaplin at some point experience the same misgivings and reluctance; and yet they still write their books. At least a dozen books on Chaplin have appeared in English since 1970, and more are on their way.

In the circumstances, therefore, I have thought the best strategy was to make a virtue of handicap, and to approach the subject obliquely through the sixty-year accumulation of literature. The object of this book has been to trace Chaplin's career as it has appeared in the mirror of opinion. The poles of that opinion, and the major landmarks in the story of Charles Chaplin as recorded in this book, were the hysterical adulation which greeted his 1921 return to Europe; and the no less hysterical hatred and vilification he suffered from a section of the American public a quarter of a century later, and which led him to spend the rest of his long life in exile in Switzerland.

The survey of opinion is necessarily selective. Mainly I have concentrated on works published in English and readily available to readers wishing amplification of particular episodes. It was irresistible, though, to include the opinions of such articulate foreign peers of Chaplin as Max Linder and Sergei Eisenstein. In other respects, when making the selection I often felt sympathy with John McCabe who claimed to have read 'virtually every book and magazine article published about Chaplin in English and French. The French material, on the whole, did not contribute much. Chaplin is almost sainted in France and understandably that kind of reverence is largely injudicial. But no matter the country, many of these exegeses make depressing reading. Some of them are metaphysical posturings that find in Chaplin's art every nuance of existence, and others too frequently crush an obvious entertainment device into a vapory metaphor pertinent only to the writer's psychological enthralments. It is always a temptation, says Robert Sherwood, to 'soar into symbolism when considering a Chaplin film'.

Endeavouring to trace Chaplin's reflected image in such various sources as the writings of critics, poets, aestheticians, fan magazines and fellow-artists, I have touched only exceptionally these crazier fringes of opinion.

The form the mirror reveals is clear enough in its outlines. Given almost every handicap a poor child in Victorian London could have, Chaplin nevertheless displayed an instinctive and irrepressible talent which already attracted attention in his teens. Within weeks of his first appearance in films audiences had picked him out; within a few months, so had the critics. In a couple of years his work attracted the word 'art' for the first time to the lowly form of film comedy; and he was being compared with Shakespeare, Dickens, Aristophanes. By the twenties he had been elevated even beyond such comparisons. He is, rhapsodized Alexander Woollcott, 'the foremost artist of the world ... His like has not passed this way before, and we shall not see his like again.'

In the long run Woollcott was right certainly few people in the twenties and thirties seriously disputed it. But the bigger they are, the harder they fall; and when, in the paranoia of the Cold War era, a powerful section of opinion turned against Chaplin it was ensured that his fall from grace should be a hard one indeed.

The world outside America still offered him warmth and adulation, and America herself was eventually to try to make amends. Time effected a natural reaction in critical opinion. Doubt or distaste over his final films made many critics look back with scepticism over his earlier achievements. Most notably in England, Chaplin went out of fashion: the partisan felt that his adulation had unfairly eclipsed the achievements of others like Keaton or Lloyd, who were now – unfairly to their own reputations – used as sticks to beat the cast-out former favourite. The human frailties of the man – the touches of vanity and egotism innocently revealed in his own writings – were irrelevantly used to invalidate the creation.

Today perhaps we have seen the tide turn. Even in Britain, new audiences approach the old films with an openness and directness of response that intervening generations had forgotten. The proliferation of new books, the promise of stage musicals and films is evidence of renewed interest in the man, and perhaps also in his creation. And when he died, on Christmas Day 1977, the whole world recognized that – whatever else had ever been said about him – Chaplin had created in the silhouette of his Tramp the most universal representation of foolish, fallible mankind that human art had ever achieved.

By the same author
Keaton
Hollywood in the Twenties
The Great Funnies
World Cinema

Translations
Luis Buñuel: A Critical Biography by Francisco Aranda
Cinema in Revolution by Schnitzer & Martin

Self-Portrait – I

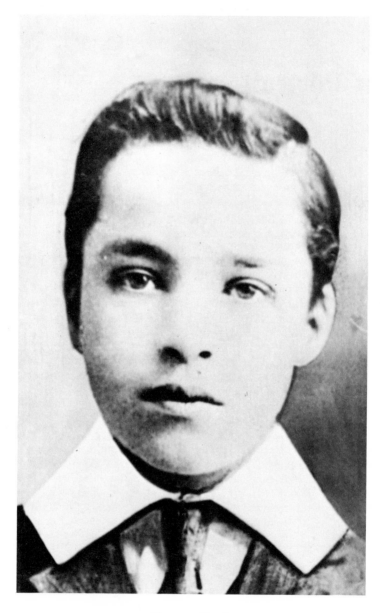

The young Chaplin

Self-Portrait – I

Even without any of his other creative achievements, Charles Chaplin would have earned a niche for himself in autobiographical literature with the early chapters of his book *My Autobiography*, published in 1964, when he was seventy-five years old. Chaplin's literary style is distinctive and could never have been wholly reproduced by literary ghosts and publishers' editors. In his youth, compensating for a sporadic formal education, he had set out with a passion to educate himself, and used to say that he made a point of studying the dictionary and learning one new word every day. In consequence no doubt he had a heightened pleasure in words and used them with vigour and colour. Some words, like 'ineffable', clearly had special relish for him.

The first hundred and fifty pages of *My Autobiography* are remarkable for their incomparably vivid impressions of poverty in a turn-of-the-century London in which both Dickensian vitality and Dickensian misery persisted side by side; they recapture, too, the exhilaration experienced in first discovering and exploring those rich talents which were to take him so far from the unpromising origins.

These were memories, of course, which would impress themselves indelibly on any youngster, but Chaplin recalled things with a peculiar acuteness – as for instance his recollection of when he first learned to write his name, 'Chaplin': 'The word fascinated me and looked like me, I thought.' He concludes a thrillingly evocative description of a ride on the top of a horse-bus from Lambeth to Westminster, presumably in the nineties, with the telling reflection, 'From such trivia I believe my soul was born'.

The story of his childhood is full of terrible scenes of poverty and its humiliations, life in institutions, the harrowing experience of watching his young mother declining into madness. Yet the most poignant passage in the book is rather the description of a rare, snatched moment of happiness in the darkest days of his infancy. Mrs Chaplin had been forced to throw herself and her two sons, Sydney and Charles, on to the mercy of the parochial authorities. She had gone into the Lambeth workhouse; the boys were sent to the Hanwell Schools for Orphans and Destitute Children, some twelve miles out of London (Charles remembered the drive there through the countryside in a horse-drawn bakery van with a kind of nostalgic pleasure). After a couple of months, Mrs Chaplin, eager to see her children again, decided on the ruse of applying for their discharge with the intention of entering them again into the Hanwell Schools the same evening – which in fact she did.

The bedraggled little family met in the early morning: 'Mother, Sydney and I looked a crumpled sight as we ambled out through the workhouse gates.' They had nowhere else to go, so they spent the morning in Kennington Park. Out of nine pence which Sydney had saved and kept tied in a handkerchief, they bought half a pound of cherries. The three of them passed the morning eating these and playing catch-ball with a ball that Sydney improvised out of an old sheet of newspaper tied with string. At noon they spent the rest of the money on a twopenny teacake, a penny bloater and two halfpenny cups of tea, which were shared between them. Then they went back to the park where the boys played while their mother sat crocheting.

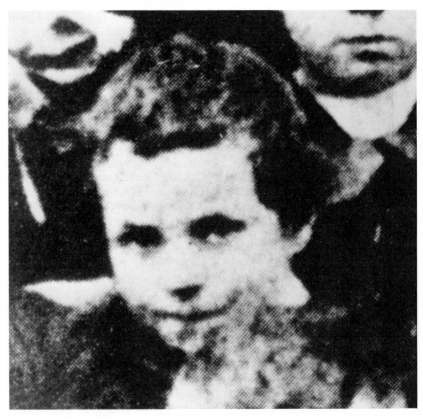

Charles Chaplin at about seven when a pupil at the Hanwell Schools

At the end of the day, the innocently guileful Mrs Chaplin led her children back to the workhouse, just in time for tea, and to the great annoyance of the authorities who had to go through all the admission procedures (including steam fumigation of the children's clothes). In this little anecdote, as Chaplin recalls it, we can see the roots of the poignant feeling Chaplin retained for his mother to the end of her life, as well as of the characteristic proximity, in all his work, of comedy and pathos.

Critics at the time of its appearance and later writers have tended to admire Chaplin's description of his early life (it was in fact subsequently published separately by The Bodley Head as *My Early Life*) while admitting disappointment with the later sections of the book which often spend much more time on descriptions of life as a world-wide celebrity than on illuminations of the creative process. Some writers, however, have sought to cast doubt on the early chapters too, sceptical of memories still so detailed and vivid sixty or seventy years after the event. Among the sceptics are Chaplin's most scholarly and least sympathetic chroniclers, Raoul Sobel and David Francis in their *Chaplin, Genesis of a Clown* (1977), whose gravest doubts apply precisely to 'the section devoted to his early life. Many vital questions are raised only to be tossed aside. Facts are surrounded with a thick fog of sentiment. Dates are scarce. To try to keep a running time-scale while reading *My Autobiography* is rather like having to navigate by the stars on an overcast night. By the time one reaches the next break in the clouds the boat may be miles off course. Certain enigmas are not even hinted at. For example there is still no explanation as to why his birth is not recorded in Somerset House ...'

Sobel and Francis quote a single instance of Chaplin's departure from fact, his very circumstantial treatment of his father's funeral, how it was paid for by a visiting Uncle Albert from Africa to save the family the humiliation of accepting charity from the Variety Artists' Benevolent Fund, and how it took place on a mournful drizzly day, 'with all the necessary middle-class trappings of grief'. In fact, as Sobel and Francis have discovered from investigation at Somerset House, the elder Chaplin was buried in a common or pauper's grave in Lambeth Cemetery.

'What made Chaplin go to such lengths to avoid the reality? It could have been his need to dramatize, but then it might be argued that a pauper's funeral gives more scope for the tragic muse than a standard burial. Might it be that he was never there, that he had not the slightest interest in seeing his father interred? Perhaps Mr Chaplin had been completely disowned by everyone and his son was ashamed to admit it years later. Perhaps he wasn't his father after all ... and so on'. There could be simpler explanations of this and other testable variations from simple fact: perhaps Chaplin had, as the years went by, supplemented his own vague memory (he was twelve at the time, and the trauma of such an event could as readily erase it from the mind as etch it in recollection) with wishful family lore supplied by his cousins. In the view of Sobel and Francis though, 'the shadow this kind of flaw casts over the rest of the book cannot be ignored'.*

Perhaps not; but where facts and chronology can be checked (and it must be admitted that the early records of a family as humble as the Chaplins are necessarily more sparse than those of grander folk) the accuracy of Chaplin's remembrance is often very much more striking than its errors. Often, indeed, the little errors actually seem to confirm the fidelity of Chaplin's record. When, for example, he remembers a kindly stage manager at the Prince of Wales Theatre in 1905 as 'Mr Postant' while reference to records shows he was actually 'Mr Postance' it does suggest that Chaplin has depended on his own memory rather than reconstruction by research in old programmes; and that the memory deceived him only in detail. In short, the checkable facts are rarely at the sort of variance which Raoul Sobel and David Francis have claimed in the case of the funeral; and where things are not checkable, and we are obliged to rely on Chaplin, he is more creditable than most old men remembering.

Perhaps, they suggest, 'the core is missing' because Chaplin's early life might have been 'more conventional and dull than he cares to reveal'. There is something a trifle heartless about their conclusion that 'Of course, there must have been periods of near-starvation when his mother was in the asylum and his brother at sea; moments of despair, of loneliness, hopelessness, of biting shame, but they did not last for ever ...' Chaplin seems to have gone out of his way to suppress any suggestion that in his early years he found anything to laugh about, which could not have been true'.

Allowing for the absence of dates (some of which can be retrieved; and were retrieved by Sobel and Francis in their biographical chronology) Chaplin's 1964 autobiography is the most substantial single source for the story of his early life.

The story began with his birth on April 16th 1889, in South London, most probably (for even here there is uncertainty) in East Lane, Walworth. His father was a modestly successful comic singer on the music halls, well enough known to top the bill in provincial theatres and to figure on the illustrated lithographic music sheets of the nineties. It is hard from the pictures to judge his height, but he seems to have been a well-built man, with a very vague likeness to his son, whose name he shared. Poor Chaplin Senior however was to succumb to the occupational disease of the music halls – the bar was the only place to go between appearances, and the managements expected that the artists by their presence there would attract the patrons to drink along with them. He died at only 37 in 1901, bequeathing to young Charles a lifelong horror of intemperance.

Chaplin's mother was a soubrette on the halls; but very little record remains of her career. In his book *My Life in Pictures* (1974), a kind of illustrated supplement to the autobiography, Chaplin illustrates a torn handbill for a variety entertainment at the Hatcham Liberal Club in New Cross, which lists among the artistes Miss Lily Chaplin; otherwise we have only her son's word for her talents and appearances as a singer. Her real name was Hannah

---

*Subsequent research establishes Chaplin's accuracy: his father *was* buried in a pauper's grave but Uncle Albert paid other funeral costs.

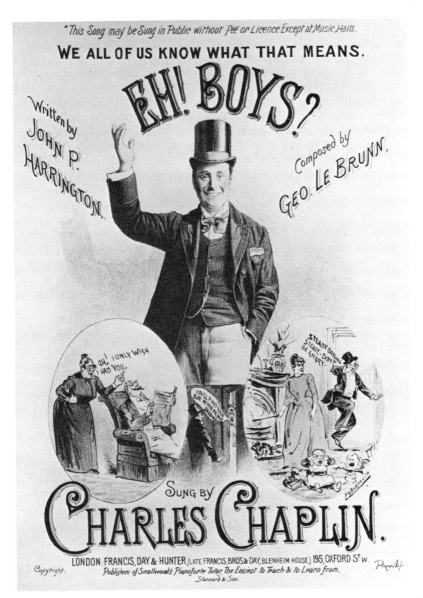

Chaplin's father, also Charles Chaplin, was a modestly successful music hall singer, popular enough to be featured on music covers. This song dates from 1895.

Hill, and she was born in 1865, the daughter of a shoe-maker. Grandfather Hill was Irish; Grandmother Hill, Chaplin proudly claimed, was half-Spanish and half-gypsy, which he believed explained his own looks. The Chaplin family seem to be of Huguenot descent: the name derives from the word *capeline* (Fr. a mailed hood). Of the wildly contradictory evidence relating to the possible Jewish element in Chaplin's ancestry, John McCabe pleasantly concludes 'As nearly as can be determined, Charlie Chaplin is virtually part Jewish almost most of the time'.

Hannah's personal life prompted Chaplin's endearing conclusion that 'To gauge the morals of our family by commonplace standards would be as erroneous as putting a thermometer in boiling water'. Hannah, whose elder sister Kate was also a soubrette, had, so it was related, gone off to South Africa with a Mr Hawkes, a Jewish bookmaker, and returned the following year, 1886, with a baby, Charlie's half-brother Sydney. Shortly afterwards she married Charles Chaplin Senior. In 1889 Charles was born; but before he was three his parents had separated, and in 1892 Hannah bore a child, Wheeler, by the music hall singer Leo Dryden. Many years later Wheeler Dryden was to join his half-brother in the film studios: he was associate producer of *Limelight* and also plays the role of a doctor in the film.

According to Charles his mother's career as a music hall singer stumbled on despite her deteriorating health. His stage debut, according to his own account, was an outcome of his mother's growing frailty. Around 1894, when he was five, he says, his mother had taken him with her to the Canteen, Aldershot, where she was appearing under her stage name of Lily Harley.

'I remember standing in the wings when Mother's voice cracked and went into a whisper. The audience began to laugh and sing falsetto and to make catcalls. It was all vague and I did not quite understand what was going on. But the noise increased until Mother was obliged to walk off the stage. When she came into the wings she was very upset and argued with the stage manager who, having seen me perform before Mother's friends, said something about letting me go on in her place.'

He was led on to the stage and sang Gus Elen's popular music hall song, ''E don't know Where 'E Are'. To his delight the rough audience, mostly soldiers, were so pleased that they threw money on to the stage. They were even more amused when he announced that he would interrupt the performance to retrieve the money; and then went on to dance and do more imitations of his mother ('Riley, Riley, that's the boy to beguile ye'). 'I was quite at home.'

Soon after this Hannah Chaplin, physically weak and mentally failing, became unable either economically or temperamentally to cope with ordinary life and two young sons. Charles and Sydney were shifted around in public institutions, and for a while were given into the care of their father and his mistress, whom Charles Chaplin describes with a mixture of detestation and pity. As soon as he was old enough, Sydney enrolled in a naval school, and from then on only intermittently returned to his mother and brother, generally able to bring them some little economic support.

Charles appears to have spent the latter part of 1896 and 1897 in the Hanwell Schools; but by 1898 Mrs Chaplin's health and circumstances seem to have looked up somewhat, and she was reunited with her young son. In the summer of that year Chaplin's professional career began in earnest. He joined a troupe of juvenile entertainers, The Eight Lancashire Lads, formed by a John Willie Jackson whose own family supplied most of the act (one of the lads was in fact a lass, with cropped hair and knickerbockers).

The tour with the Eight Lancashire Lads seems to have given the ten-year-old Charlie intermittent work for more than a year. The act got good bookings around the numerous music halls of London and the provinces; and the child Chaplin often found himself on the same bills as some of the great vaudeville stars of the time, like Dan Leno, Marie Lloyd and George Robey. At Christmas 1900 some of the Lads, Chaplin said, were engaged for the London Hippodrome pantomime. He claims to have created a furore one night with a piece of improvised business: playing a pantomime cat, he backed up to the wings and lifted his leg in a most unfeline way.

The run of the pantomime ended in April 1901, and Chaplin appears not to have returned to the Lancashire Lads. The rest of that year must have been bleak. In May his father died, and soon afterwards his mother, who was never again fully to recover her mental stability, was admitted to Cane Hill Asylum for the Insane.

In July 1903, Chaplin landed a rewarding little part as Sam the Newsboy in *A Romance of Cockayne*, by H. A. Saintsbury. The play lasted only a little more than a fortnight; but then Saintsbury cast him as Billy the page in *Sherlock Holmes*, which toured for eighteen months until December 1904. Chaplin was clearly a success in his role of Billy since he was retained for three more tours of the play, even though the principals had changed; and when the distinguished American actor William Gillette required a Billy for a one-acter *The Painful Predicament of Sherlock Holmes*, which he was playing as support to his own new comedy *Clarice* at the Duke of York's, Charles Chaplin was summoned to London. *Clarice* failed; Gillette hastily replaced it with a revival of *Sherlock Holmes*; and Charles was back in his own part. The London production and a subsequent tour of the play kept him in work until March 1906.

After this it was something of a come-down to return from the legitimate theatre to the music halls and another comedy act, *Casey's Court*, a long-running juvenile troupe formed by Will Murray. The tour in which Charles Chaplin was employed between May 1906 and July 1907 was called 'Casey's Circus'.

Meanwhile, however, Charles' elder brother Sydney had abandoned the sea – he had been working on passenger liners – to establish himself as a variety artist. By 1907 Sydney was playing leading roles in one of the several sketch companies organised by the music hall impresario Fred Karno. In

Duke of York's Theatre
ST MARTIN'S LANE W C

Proprietors ... ... Mr & Mrs FRANK WYATT
Sole Lessee and Manager ... ... CHARLES FROHMAN

CHARLES FROHMAN PRESENTS
A DRAMA IN FOUR ACTS
BY A. CONAN DOYLE
AND WILLIAM GILLETTE
ENTITLED

SHERLOCK HOLMES

BEING A HITHERTO UNPUBLISHED EPISODE
IN THE CAREER OF THE GREAT DETECTIVE
AND SHOWING HIS CONNECTION WITH THE

STRANGE CASE OF MISS FAULKNER

CHARACTERS IN THE PLAY		COMPANY APPEARING IN THE CAST
SHERLOCK HOLMES ...		WILLIAM GILLETTE
DOCTOR WATSON		KENNETH RIVINGTON
JOHN FORMAN		EUGENE MAYEUR
SIR EDWARD LEIGHTON		REGINALD DANCE
COUNT VON STAHLBURG		FREDERICK MORRIS
PROFESSOR MORIARTY		GEORGE SUMNER
JAMES LARRABEE		FRANCIS CARLYLE
SIDNEY PRINCE		QUINTON McPHERSON
ALFRED BASSICK		WILLIAM H. DAY
JIM CRAIGIN		CHRIS WALKER
THOMAS LEARY		HENRY WALTERS
"LIGHTFOOT" McTAGUE ...		WALTER DISON
JOHN		THOMAS QUINTON
PARSONS		G. MERTON
BILLY		CHARLES CHAPLIN
ALICE FAULKNER ...		MARIE DORO
MRS. FAULKNER		DE OLIA WEBSTER
MADGE LARRABEE		ADELAIDE PRINCE
THERESE		SYBIL CAMPBELL
MRS. SMEEDLEY		ETHEL LORRIMORE

THE PLACE IS LONDON
THE TIME TEN YEARS AGO

FIRST ACT—DRAWING ROOM AT THE LARRABEES'—EVENING
SECOND ACT—SCENE I—PROFESSOR MORIARTY'S
UNDERGROUND OFFICE—MORNING
SCENE II—SHERLOCK HOLMES' APARTMENTS
IN BAKER STREET—EVENING
THIRD ACT—THE STEPNEY GAS CHAMBER—MIDNIGHT
FOURTH ACT—DOCTOR WATSON'S CONSULTING ROOM KENSINGTON—THE
FOLLOWING EVENING

SCENERY BY ERNEST GROS   INCIDENTAL MUSIC BY WILLIAM FURST

INTERMISSIONS
Between the 1st and 2nd Acts, 9 minutes
Between the 2nd and 3rd Acts, 7 minutes
Between the 3rd and 4th Acts, 8 minut s

MATINEE every Saturday at 2.15 o'clock

BUSINESS MANAGER—JAMES W MATHEWS   ACTING MANAGER—ROBERT M EBERLE
STAGE MANAGER—WILLIAM FOSTANCE   MUSICAL DIRECTOR—JOHN CROOK

ICES TEA AND COFFEE can be had of the Attendants

The youthful Chaplin as a legitimate actor: programme for the 1905 production of Sherlock Holmes, *with Chaplin as Billy.*

September of that year he persuaded Karno to engage his younger brother at a salary of £2.10s a week.

Chaplin's debut with the Karno organization (he reckoned that Karno kept as many as eighteen companies on the road at one time) was as a rag-and-bone man in the sketch *London – Suburbia* in which Sydney was currently starring. Promoted to the role of comic villain, attempting to bribe the goalie, in *The Football Match*, his ability to improvise gags and capture an audience was instantly evident and aroused the jealous hostility of the principal Karno star, Harry Weldon, who created and played the role of Stiffy the Goalkeeper. Within a few months of joining the company, Chaplin himself was playing this leading role at the London Coliseum. Later in 1909 he was selected for the troupe which played at the Folies Bergères in Paris – the silent pantomime of the Karno sketches made them eminently exportable

Chaplin as a member of the Casey's Circus company, about 1906. The proprietor of the act, Will Murray is on Chaplin's right.

9

ƒRED KARNO'S

ℂOMPANIES.

"HIS MAJESTY'S GUESTS."
"SATURDAY TO MONDAY."
"THE DANDY THIEVES."
MUMMING BIRDS."
"EARLY BIRDS."
"JAIL BIRDS."
"THE DIVING BIRDS
"THE THIRSTY FIRST.'
"MOSES & SON.'
"HILARITY.'
NEW WOMAN'S CLUB. '
"THUMBS DOWN."
'CINDERELLA," &c.

Sole Proprietor and Director   ..   ..   Mr. FRED KARNO
General Manager and Producer ...   .   Mr. HERBERT DARNLEY

Advertisement for Fred Karno's companies, c.1906.

– in the most celebrated and successful of all the Karno sketches, *Mumming Birds*. The sketch presented a stage within the stage, on which appeared a succession of stock music hall acts, each more dreadful than the last. Chaplin's role was as a member of the audience, a drunken toff whose obstreperous antics eventually disrupted the show. He substantially transferred *Mumming Birds* to the screen in his two-reel film *A Night at the Show*, conveying what is perhaps the best impression of the Karno approach to comedy and revealing the debt – which he was always ready to acknowledge – to Karno's training.

In the years that followed Chaplin played leading roles in most of the Karno sketches, including one created by his brother, *Skating* (this again undoubtedly inspired *The Rink*). In 1910 Karno offered him the leading role in *Jimmy the Fearless or the Boy 'ero*, but Chaplin refused it – only to think better of the matter after he saw the role a success in the hands of another youngster, Stan Jefferson, who was later to be better known as Stan Laurel. Laurel told John McCabe, who was to be biographer to both artists, 'I didn't feel bitter about it. For me, Charlie was, is, and will be always the greatest comedian in the world. I thought he should have played it to begin with'. Laurel also felt that the role of the working lad who dreams of heroic adventures, only to be wakened to hard reality, often influenced Chaplin's later creations.

In the autumn of 1910 Chaplin and Laurel were both chosen for a Karno company to tour the United States. The whole company questioned Karno's choice of *The Wow Wows*, a rather local skit on masonic and other secret

The Karno sketch company during Chaplin's first American tour, 1911. Chaplin is at the left of the group, Stan Jefferson (Stan Laurel) and Albert Austin in the highest position at the back. The troupe is in costume for The Wow-Wows.

societies; and it seems certain that it was only Chaplin's skill on stage and in inventing business which rescued the show. The Karno troupe certainly had greater applause when they presented as an alternative *Mumming Birds*, retitled for the States *A Night in an English Music Hall*.

The company returned to England in the early summer of 1912, in time for Chaplin to take off for some tours of France and the Channel Islands. The return home was not entirely happy: Mrs Chaplin was back in an asylum; Sydney Chaplin had married and given up the flat which the boys had rented together as a home. After arranging for his mother to go into a private hospital, Chaplin seems rather gladly to have embarked in December 1912 on a second Karno tour of the United States. It was during this trip that he was approached by Adam Kessel Jr and Charles O. Bauman with a proposition to join the Keystone Comedy Film company at a salary of 150 dollars a week. This was double his salary with the Karno Company but Chaplin – distinctly doubtful about the move in any case – bargained with Kessel and Bauman, asking for two hundred dollars a week. Finally he settled for a year's contract and a salary rising from 150 dollars a week to 175 dollars after three months.

Poster for the second American tour of Karno's comedians. The portraits from top are Amy Minister (Mrs Alf Reeves), Alf Reeves, Chaplin, ?, Chaplin and Stanley Jefferson, later to be better known as Stan Laurel.

Loyally, however, he insisted on working out his contract with the Karno Company; and made his last stage performance at the Empress Theatre Kansas City on 28th November 1913. (It is one of the small errors of Chaplin's recollection that his autobiography gives the date as September.) From Kansas City he entrained for California and his new job.

Chaplin's earliest press notices have been frequently reprinted by successive biographers, but it is perhaps necessary to record them once again here, to complete the portrait reflected in the opinions of three quarters of a century. Five days after his first appearance in *Jim: A Romance of Cockayne* the theatrical paper *The Era* remarked, 'Of the others taking part in the play, mention should be made of ... Master Charles Chaplin, who, as a newsboy known as Sam, showed promise'. The following week *The Era* decided to praise him again: 'Master Charles Chaplin is a broth of a boy as Sam, the newspaper boy, giving a most realistic picture of the cheeky, honest, loyal, self-reliant, philosophical street Arab who haunts the regions of Cockayne.' The child seems, indeed, to have been father of the man.

Chaplin says in his autobiography that he still remembered, word for word, the review of the *London Topical Times*, and that it read: 'But there is one redeeming feature, the part of Sammy, a newspaper boy, a smart London street Arab, much responsible for the comic part. Although hackneyed and old-fashioned, Sammy was made vastly amusing by Master Charles Chaplin, a bright and vigorous child actor. I have never heard of the boy before, but I hope to hear great things of him in the near future.' Sydney, he recalls, bought a dozen copies.

The Era again praised him for Billy in the Gillette *Sherlock Holmes*: 'The part of Billy is well played by Mr Charles Chaplin, who succeeds in making the smart pageboy a prime favourite with the audience.'

By 1905 Chaplin was clearly an established actor. He had an agent, paid to have his professional 'card' in *The Stage* and somehow managed to earn an entry in *The Green Room Book*, the forerunner of *Who's Who in the Theatre* and much shorter and more selective about those who were included than its successor.

Chaplin began to earn notices for his work with Karno principally in the United States. He merited a special mention in every review in local papers in the towns where the company appeared across the States. *Variety*, then still fairly new to its role as the bible of show business, didn't find *The Wow-Wows* very funny, but thought Chaplin 'typically English, the sort of comedian that American audiences seem to like, although unaccustomed to. His manner is quiet and easy and he goes about his work in a devil-may-care manner, in direct contrast to the twenty-minutes-from-a-cemetery make-up he employs.

'The make-up and the manner in themselves are funny. That is what will have to carry *The Wow-Wows* over, if it goes that way. Chaplin will do all right for America ...'

Employers and Mentors

Aside from his natural and instinctive gifts, Chaplin had the benefit of a schooling in comedy such as could hardly have been bettered at any time in the whole history of entertainment. He passed from a seven-year apprenticeship with the unchallenged father of stage slapstick in Britain to the guidance of the founding father of American screen comedy. His enduring regard for both Fred Karno and Mack Sennett was evidence of his gratitude to these early mentors.

Karno (1866–1941) was born Frederick Westcott, the son of an Exeter cabinet maker. After a variety of jobs, including coster, factory labourer and bricklayer's mate, he worked for a plumber, and conceived the idea of becoming an acrobat while mending pipes in a gymnasium. He started his theatrical career as a girl gymnast, then joined a circus where he made his eventual speciality comic pantomime sketches. In time he progressed to producing his own sketches for the music hall stage, and eventually had several companies permanently on tour, and a whole repertory of sketches, *Jail Birds*, *Mumming Birds*, *Early Birds*, *The Football Match*, *The Wow-Wows* among them. At first Karno sketches were played entirely in pantomime – clearly a useful discipline for future film artists of the teens and twenties of the century – though eventually a degree of dialogue was introduced.

To maintain and supply his companies, Karno adapted two or three houses in Camberwell Road as his Fun Factory, where his writers and gag men worked, costumes and props were made, sets were built, and from which buses (horse-drawn at first; later motorised) drove off each day carrying the troupes to London and suburban music halls.

In private life Karno seems to have been a remarkably unpleasant man, particularly in his treatment of wives, mistresses and other women. Chaplin himself admitted that he 'could be cynical and cruel to anyone he disliked. Because he liked me I had never seen that side of him, but he could indeed be most crushing in a vulgar way'. Karno's employees seem however to have held him in awed respect. It is notable that in his autobiography Chaplin refers to him always as 'Mr Karno'. Stan Laurel, who was more or less contemporary with Chaplin as a Karno player told John McCabe of the

Fred Karno in the office of his 'Fun Factory' in Camberwell.

Fred Karno's 'Fun Factory' in Vaughan Road, Camberwell.

invention and polish that characterized the work of the Karno companies: 'No language was necessary because the acting of the troupe was vivid and expressive enough to bring laughter from any race. All of the pieces we did, as I remember them, were cruel and boisterous, filled with acrobatic humour and low, knockabout comedy. Each man working for Karno had to have perfect timing and had to know the peculiarities of everyone else in the cast so that we could, collectively, achieve a cast tempo.' Karno's methods of bringing the best out of his artists seem not to have been over-subtle. 'During a performance of one of his comedies,' Chaplin recalled; 'if he did not like a comedian he would stand in the wings and hold his nose and give an audible raspberry.'

Stan Laurel revealed, however, that one of the most important lessons imparted by Karno was the value of introducing pathos into laughter. In the midst of rehearsals of the most reckless slapstick he would call out, 'Keep it wistful, gentlemen, keep it *wistful* as well. That's hard to do but we want sympathy with the laughter. Wistful!' Recording this, John McCabe adds, 'Charlie Chaplin, one might say, was born wistful. In this and other ways he ranked first among the Karno comedians'.

What evidence we have of Karno's impressions of Chaplin – apart from the very evident fact that he saw him as one, at least, of his star employees – comes, somewhat at second hand, from a 1939 biography by Edwin Adeler and Con West. Karno himself, by this time fallen on hard times and keeping a little off-licence wine store in which he had been set up by the Variety Artists' Benevolent Fund, was clearly their principal informant – and a great deal more charitable to himself than those who confided their recollections to a late biographer, J. P. Gallaher (*Fred Karno, Master of Mirth and Tears*, 1971).

Adeler and West claimed that theirs was the 'full, true and authorised version of the Karno–Chaplin relations', though it reveals rather less than Chaplin's own account with which, in essentials it agrees. (One of Chaplin's more unpleasant side-lights on Karno's character is the story of how, when he asked 'the Guv'nor' for a raise in salary, Karno had anticipated him by having a man at the other end of the phone to assert that he was a theatre manager and that his audiences considered Chaplin 'stank').

When Chaplin was brought to him by brother Sydney, Karno thought 'he looked under-nourished and frightened as though he expected me to raise my hand to hit him. I thought he looked much too shy to do any good in the theatre, particularly in the knockabout comedies that were my specialty.' Karno quickly perceived Chaplin's quality, and – unusually with his employees – clearly took a liking to the lad. Karno's first biographers recall, however, that Charlie was selected for the American tour because Karno did not want to run the risk of losing Sydney, whom he saw as the more valuable star, to the movies, which were already proving voracious for talent. He recalled that he lectured him on the opportunities he had given him and urged, 'Now, look here, Charlie. I do hope you won't do the same as the others'.

'Have no fears for me, guv'nor' Chaplin replied, according to Karno's version of the story; 'I can't see myself acting before a camera.'

'To prevent misunderstanding,' wrote Adeler and West, clearly echoing Karno himself, 'it should here be pointed out that Fred Karno does not claim, and never has claimed to have "made" Charlie Chaplin. Managers don't make artistes – though, through sheer crass stupidity, they often unmake them by robbing them of opportunity, or by putting square pegs into round holes. What Fred Karno did was to set the boy on the right road, to fan the faint glow of his genius till it flamed up; to give him the parts that suited him, and the chances to make good.'

Years afterwards, when Karno visited Chaplin in Hollywood he was flattered that the great comedian greeted him with 'Do you know, I feel almost as over-awed by you as I always was'. He cancelled all his engagements to entertain Karno for the day, and presented him to Marion Davies and to Irving Berlin who crowned the older man's happiness by exclaiming 'Not *the* Fred Karno'. Karno's years of success were over, however. He was engaged as a producer at the Hal Roach studio; but his irascibility and growing insecurity cut short his American venture. Later attempts at film production (including a couple of two-reelers with the Crazy Gang) also came to grief; and when Fred Karno died he left only a little over forty pounds.

Mack Sennett (1890–1960) was also to see his own star fade and to end his life in comparative obscurity; but when Chaplin joined his company he was at the peak of his career. Sennett, wrote James Agee, 'took his comics out of music halls, burlesque, vaudeville, circuses and limbo and through them he tapped in on that great pipeline of horsing and miming which runs back unbroken through the fairs of the Middle Ages at least to Ancient Greece. He added all that he himself had learned about the large and spurious gesture, the late decadence of the Grand Manner, as a stage-struck boy in East Berlin, Connecticut and as a frustrated singer and actor. The only thing he claims to have invented is the pie in the face, and he insists, "Anyone who tells you he has discovered something new is a fool or a liar or both"'. (Ironically enough, English writers are inclined to claim for Karno the distinction of transforming the custard pie into a missile.)

Sennett, whose real name was Michael Sinnott, was born of Irish parents. An introduction from Calvin Coolidge, then a lawyer in Sennett's small home town, earned him an introduction to Marie Dressler; and an introduction from Marie Dressler gained him an interview with David Belasco, the great actor-manager, in New York. Belasco advised him to give up all thoughts of serious drama and to pursue his comic talents; Sennett knocked around for a few years as a super in operas and a comedian in music hall sketch companies before finding work at the Biograph Studios in New York, where the principal director was D. W. Griffith. He assiduously studied Griffith's techniques, and was rewarded by becoming a director in his own right. Soon he was Biograph's principal comedy director. Wheedling, says Agee, 'his financing out of a couple of ex-bookies to whom he was already in debt', Sennett established the Keystone Studios. The ex-bookies were Adam Kessel and Charles O. Bauman, who in 1913, at Sennett's recommendation, engaged the twenty-four-year-old Charles Chaplin.

When he came to write his own somewhat imaginative memoirs, in collaboration with Cameron Shipp, Sennett reminisced at length about the year that Chaplin spent in his studios. His first sight of the English comedian was when with Mabel Normand, his favourite star and life-long love, he chanced into the American Music Hall at 42nd Street and 8th Avenue, New York. Although Miss Normand liked Chaplin's style Sennett admits he was less convinced: 'That Limey make-up and costume – I don't know.' When later he felt in need of a new comedian, since his leading male comic Ford Sterling was asking for more money and he had just made the mistake of sacking Harold Lloyd because he didn't think him funny, he remembered Chaplin's name.

Or rather, he did not remember Chaplin's name but, so he claims, sent a telegram to the theatre where the Karno Company were playing, saying: 'Is there a man named Chaffin in your company or something like that stop if so will he communicate with Kessel and Bauman ...' Sennett confirms the view of Chaplin himself and everyone else who was around the studio at the time, that no-one was particularly happy about the arrival of the new

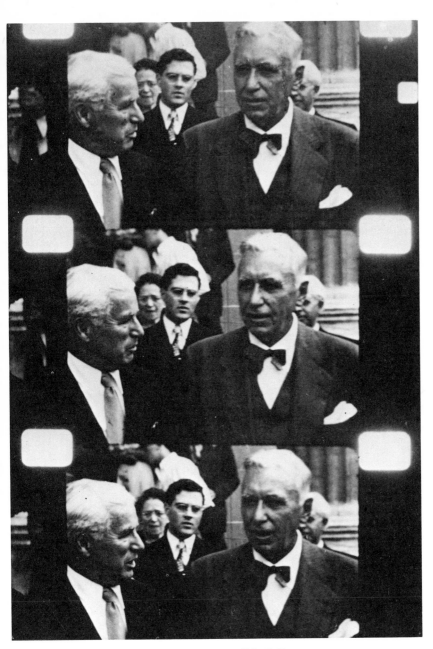

Chaplin with Mack Sennett at the funeral of D.W.Griffith, 1948.

comedian at the studios. Sennett himself was startled to find how young he was. Mabel Normand declined to work with him: 'I should say not. I don't like him so good now that I've seen him.' Chaplin himself 'was confused and plaintive. He couldn't understand what was going on, why everything went so fast'.

A fellow-comedian Chester Conklin, whom Chaplin was later to employ in his films right up to *The Great Dictator*, endeavoured to reassure him when he confided: 'I'm going to get out of this business. It's too much for me. I'll never catch on. It's too fast, I can't tell what I'm doing, or what anybody wants me to do ... The cinema is little more than a fad. It's canned drama. What audiences want is to see flesh and blood on the stage. I'm not even sure any real actor should get caught posing for the flickahs.'

Initially Sennett had grave doubts whether Chaplin was funny at all. His first film, *Making a Living* cast him as a dubious dandy, in frock coat, monocle and silk hat; the character was only vaguely defined, and Chaplin didn't like the film at all; but it made an instant impression. *The Moving Picture*

Chaplin helpfully ensures that Chester Conklin, even though trapped in the cogs of a machine, shall not miss his lunch. Modern Times *1936*

A Keystone announcement for Chaplin's first and third films for the studio, 1914.

World, an important trade magazine, reported: 'The clever player who takes the role of nervy and very nifty sharper in this picture is a comedian of the first water, who acts like one of Nature's own naturals ... People out for an evening's good time will howl.'

Chaplin's second appearance was in a five-minute piece of nonsense shot off the cuff – as the Keystone Company was often wont to do – in the foreground of a sporting event, a children's auto race. Chaplin (drawing on the memory of a bumptious local official showing off in front of a newsreel camera during a Karno tour in the Channel Islands) played a foolish little man who insistently got in the way of the newsreel cameras attempting to film the *Kid Auto Races at Venice.*

What made the film historic, however, was that Chaplin had, in a single stroke, adopted the costume that was henceforth for ever to be associated with him. Sennett quotes Conklin's version of how the costume was put together in Fatty Arbuckle's dressing room. Chaplin put on a pair of Arbuckle's immense pants, a coat that belonged to diminutive Charles Avery, a derby hat that belonged to Arbuckle's father-in-law and a pair of boots that belonged to Ford Sterling and were so much too big for Chaplin that he had to wear them on the wrong feet in order to make them stay on. A necktie, waistcoat and wigger-wagger cane of uncertain provenance completed the attire; a moustache perfected the make-up. With the costume though, came the character. '... The moment I was dressed, the clothes and the make-up made me feel the person he was. I began to know him, and by the time I walked onto the stage he was fully born. When I confronted Sennett I assumed the character and strutted about, swinging my cane and parading before him. Gags and comedy ideas went racing through my mind.'

Mabel Normand repented of her previous refusal to work with Chaplin, and became his earliest and most irresistibly vivacious leading lady. Sennett, though much of what he writes is highly coloured by hindsight, undoubtedly began, after a few more films, to appreciate Chaplin's singular talent and individual style and pace. He came to recognize that 'anything that distracted the camera's eye from Chaplin himself is likely to be a waste of celluloid.' 'We seldom used chase scenes with Chaplin', he declares; 'Chaplin was often – almost always – a fugitive, but he was a furtive fugitive; he hid and peeped'.

When Chaplin's year's contract was up, he left Keystone. Legend has it that Sennett was not prepared to raise his salary competitively. Sennett denies the legend, claiming that he offered Chaplin half his share in Keystone; but that it was not enough. Whatever the truth, Chaplin left.

Sennett remembered: 'Chaplin was still shy and inarticulate and I do not know that he ever found a way to say to me why he thought he was different from other comedians. But he knew it.'

The Great Audience. 1914–19

Both Chaplin and his Keystone boss recalled that he reported for his first day's work, but was so appalled by the chaos and uproar of the studio that he fled back to his hotel and stayed there until Sennett called him two days later. In silent picture days studios were notoriously noisy places. At Keystone, not only was there a stock company of the rowdiest comedians in the business, but there was a constant turmoil of set-building and set-wrecking, a flurry of prop-men and wardrobe people to keep up a production schedule of half a dozen pictures a week.

Most commentators have pointed out that production methods at Keystone unconsciously revived the creative system of the *commedia dell'arte*. The inspiration was generally a chosen context – a park, a lake, a baker's, butcher's or hardware shop, backstage of a theatre, a film studio, or anywhere else that could offer the props and hazards for comedy. Within the given context the broadest story-line was laid down. After that it was up to the comedians, all developed masters of improvisation, to invent their gags and business. Among them there was the valuable stimulus of always wanting to outdo the next man in violence, extravagance and absurdity.

The pace of Keystone comedies was unvarying and hectic and aggravated by Sennett's general principal of having cameramen undercrank so that in projection the film accelerated the already breakneck speed of the comic business. This was not only exciting to the audience, but served to cover up the weaker gags. Little was thrown away at Keystone. When Chaplin first began to demonstrate his rigorous selectivity (when he won independence he was to shoot many reels of film to arrive at the few feet which satisfied him) he was considered crazily extravagant. At Keystone the aim was to use every foot of film that was shot; and Sennett even frowned on editors who rejected shot-ends. In 1913 there was still a minimum of cutting within scenes: individual scenes were regarded as tiny stage scenes, with entrance, action and exits.

Chaplin's first problem at Keystone was that the breakneck speed of action was totally in conflict with the more leisurely developed gag comedy he had learned with Karno. For their part his new colleagues simply thought him

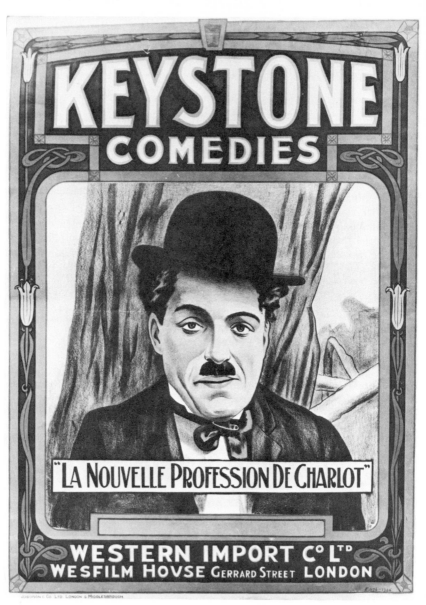

A European poster of 1914–15. If the French title La Nouvelle Profession de Charlot *actually refers to the film* His New Job, *it suggests that the European distributors were still using Keystone posters for Chaplin's first Essanay film.*

slow. The job of Keystone directors was very much to hurry things along, and to get comedians and camera in the right place. Friction was inevitable. Chaplin's first four films were directed by Henry 'Pathé' Lehrman (his nickname was acquired since he had originally conned his way into films by claiming a training in France with the Pathé Company, whereas his only prior qualifications were as a street car conductor). Lehrman was a sadistic, irascible and cocky little man, who dismissed Chaplin's suggestions and (so the comedian felt) cut his best effects out of the finished films. Four more films were directed by the elderly George Nichols. When friction between Chaplin and his directors persisted, Sennett, sometimes in collaboration with Chaplin's co-star Mabel Normand, took over. Chaplin's resentment of Mabel's somewhat high-handed supervision led to a further, though temporary rift; and with *Caught in a Cabaret*, made in April 1914, Chaplin and Normand shared director credit. It was clear that Chaplin's whole ambition was now to direct his own films. His next, *Caught in the Rain* was his first solo direction credit. After that, apart from three films co-directed with Mabel; one, *The Knockout*, in which Chaplin appears only briefly as the referee; and another, *The Fatal Mallet*, a low farce knocked up by Sennett and Mabel, Chaplin was to direct every film in which he appeared.

In all Chaplin made thirty-five films at Keystone. Since his year there included fourteen weeks spent on the production of *Tillie's Punctured Romance*, this represents an average of almost one film a week. Some, like *Caught in the Rain* were shot in an hour or two; while *The New Janitor*, with Chaplin finding his feet and demonstrating his independence, took a leisurely seventeen days, and already looked forward to his later work in its comparatively careful dramatic construction.

Most of the Keystone work, however, conforms to the studio norms of speed and slapstick, with a maximum use of knockabout, prat-falls and kicking of rears and sometimes heads. The films remain in essence dramatized comic strips. In this context, Chaplin's characteristics rather than his character emerge. The particular gait, the use of the cane, the unique method of cornering with one leg stuck out like a traffic signal, the grins, the endless tricks with the multi-purpose cane are already in evidence; but he could still step aside from the classic figure to appear in frock coat (*Mabel at the Wheel*), baker's whites (*Dough and Dynamite*), bearskin and derby (*His Prehistoric Past*); or shaven-lipped in *Tango Tangles*. At Keystone, for the first time, he played a female role – the angry wife of *A Busy Day*. 'The tramp at this stage', noted Roger Manvell, 'was a real vagabond, a compound (admits Sennett) of cruelty, venality, treachery, larceny and lechery'. Especially cruelty: Chaplin hits and kicks with the rest of them. But, Dr Manvell adds, 'The point is that Charlie carried out his nefarious business with such charm, gaiety and adroitness, while looking either innocent or pathetic, that the world responded happily to such an engaging villain'. John McCabe points out two other virtues – apart from the profitable use of the gag resources brought from Karno. In everything he does, Chaplin demonstrates that sincerity of

The Face on the Bar Room Floor *1914*.

belief and reality that is 'the difference between great acting and clever impersonation'.

In *Tillie's Punctured Romance* Chaplin took second billing to Marie Dressler, though his name now preceded that of Mabel Normand on the credits. Sennett, seeing Hollywood about to move in the direction of feature-length production, had decided to gamble on the first feature-length comedy. As a guarantee of success, he imported a major Broadway star, Marie Dressler; and after some indecision over the right vehicle decided on an adaptation of the actress's 1910 stage success *Tillie's Nightmare*, in which she had introduced the song 'Heaven Will Protect the Working Girl'.

Tillie is a heavy-weight farm-girl; Charlie is a con-man and fortune-hunter and Mabel is his jealous city girl-friend. Most of the action consists in the attempt to lay hands on Tillie's supposed legacy and in immumerable physical humiliations inflicted upon her. Marie Dressler mugs unconscionably and excessively (she has in fact the appeal and stature to get away with it); and Chaplin seized the chance to offer the contrast of the most restrained, leisurely, even poker-face comedy he had displayed up to that time in films. The film was a huge commercial success; and the notices Chaplin received consolidated the growing fame and popularity of the preceding months.

When Sennett failed to meet Chaplin's financial demands, the comedian signed a contract with Essanay – a company whose name was a play on the initial letters of the names of its founders, Charles K. Spoor and 'Broncho Billy', G. M. Anderson. The contract paid him 1250 dollars a week, with a 10,000 dollar bonus on signature, and provided for the production of one two-reel film every fortnight. In fact the fourteen films Chaplin made for Essanay took some thirteen months to complete: he was already beginning to expend much more time and care on his films and to enrich them and his own character with new elements of pathos, fantasy, irony and satire.

He found valuable new collaborators at Essanay. His cameraman, Roland Totheroh, was to stay with him as long as Chaplin worked in the United States. Totheroh understood, and never attempted to elaborate, the simple and uncluttered pictorial style which Chaplin realized provided the best stage for his performance, even after critics began to charge him with being primitive, reactionary and unimaginative in his filmic method.

The Essanay Company's stars of 1915, Francis X. Bushman, Chaplin and G. M. (Broncho Billy) Anderson.

His new leading lady, Edna Purviance, was a stenographer when he discovered her. Her fair-haired, innocently voluptuous beauty and a manner less aggressively cheeky than Normand, favoured the new element of romantic pathos that was invading Chaplin's films. Miss Purviance was to remain Chaplin's leading lady through thirty-five films and seven years; and was to adore him for the rest of her life. Chaplin repaid her by keeping her on the studio payroll long after her retirement in the early twenties, and indeed right up to her death in 1958.

The Essanay films often repeated old Keystone themes and even Karno sketches, though more elaborate in structure and gag content. The first Essanay film *His New Job*, like his fourth Keystone, *A Film Johnnie* was set in a film studio, with Charlie's presence causing the predictable havoc. Similarly *The Champion* enriched material seen in *The Knockout*; and *In the Park* (a 'quickie' by Chaplin's Essanay standards) revisited the scene of many a Keystone catastrophe. *A Woman* again lured Chaplin to female impersonation. *A Night in the Show* was frankly based on Karno's *Mumming Birds*, and remains perhaps the best available visual evidence of the Karno style.

In contrast to the Keystone lot, whose chaos had never been really sympa-

The most brilliant of several boxing sequences that appear in Chaplin's films. Chaplin is with Alan Garcia and Hank Mann. City Lights *1931.*

thetic to Chaplin's temperament, the main hazard of Essanay's Chicago studios, where Chaplin completed the first films, was the excessive sense of order and organization. On his first day Chaplin, it is said, was obliged to assert himself and his practice of writing his own material, when he was handed a script by the story editor – none other than Louella Parsons, the columnist-to-be. Chaplin requested to be transferred to California, and made several succeeding films at Broncho Billy's primitive studio at Niles. He was not happy here either, and as soon as possible moved his unit to a rented studio in a converted Los Angeles mansion. Locations around Niles, however, provided the romantically rural look of *The Tramp*, his most sophisticated film to that time (April 1915) and the first clear demonstration of his special quality of commingled laughter and sentiment.

The quality was still more evident in *The Bank*, released four months later. The story-line is elaborate: the humble janitor, like Jimmy the Fearless, dreams heroic dreams of worsting the bank robbers and winning the heart of the pretty cashier, only to wake to hard reality, embracing not his heroine, but the mop. While Chaplin was introducing much greater depths of feeling and sentiment into his films, and elaborating their story structures, his gag invention was as prolific and rich as at any time in his career. James Agee, his most loving critic, particularly admired a scene in *A Night Out* where Chaplin and cross-eyed Ben Turpin are playing drunks. 'He is supine as a sled. Turpin himself is so drunk he can hardly drag him. Chaplin comes quietly to realize how well he is being served by his struggling pal, and with a royally delicate gesture plucks and savours a flower'. Chaplin films were making fortunes for Essanay; and they were costing more also. Chaplin was already astounding his colleagues and employers by the pains he would take in rehearsing and shooting a scene; and the amount of film he would use before he was satisfied. There were other extravagances: for *Shanghaied* the studio bought and blew up a small boat.

Essanay, nevertheless could not face up to the cost of renewing Chaplin's contract: Sydney Chaplin, now acting as his brother's manager, sought half a million dollars to cover twelve two-reel pictures and to include a $150,000 bonus. After Chaplin moved on from the company he sued them unsuccessfully for extending one of his last films, *Charlie Chaplin's Burlesque on Carmen* (Cecil B. De Mille's *Carmen* and another version starring Theda Bara were currently in the news) to four reels by the addition of new material involving Ben Turpin. Essanay also fabricated a new film, *Triple Trouble* out of sections from *Police*, *Work* and an unfinished film called *Life*, which was said to be based on Chaplin's recollections of his own hard London boyhood.

Chaplin marked the end of his Essanay contract by travelling to New York for the first holiday since he had left Karno. Only the spectacle of the crowds who mobbed his train at stops along the route finally brought home to him how great a celebrity he had become in little more than two years in pictures. In New York he signed a much publicised contract with the Mutual

Film Company, which was to provide him with a weekly salary of $10,000 a week and a bonus of $150,000. He was to take eighteen months to make twelve two-reelers for Mutual. The average cost, including Chaplin's salary, was considerably in excess of the average feature-length production of the period.

Chaplin later called the Mutual period the happiest of his life. He took with him Edna Purviance and the cameraman Totheroh, and formed a regular little company around him at his new studio (called the Lone Star), including Albert Austin and Eric Campbell, the former a Karno veteran. Campbell, Chaplin's most perfect foil as gigantic, beetle-browed heavy, appeared in all but one of the Mutual comedies, but then tragically lost his life in a car accident shortly after completing *The Adventurer* late in 1917.

The film in which Campbell did not appear was *One A.M.* an astonishing *tour-de-force* which is virtually a solo (Albert Austin appears briefly at the start of the film as a taxi driver). Charlie plays a swell returning home drunk, and battling with such hazards of the inebriate state as locks and keys, animal rugs, furniture, fish and a Murphy bed. *The Pawnshop* also includes a memorable, prolonged solo sequence in which Chaplin, as the pawnbroker's assistant performs a brilliant autopsy on an alarm clock proffered in pawn by a hapless customer (Albert Austin again).

Reworkings of the same subjects reveal how fast was Chaplin's progress. The development from Keystone's *A Film Johnnie* to Essanay's *His New Job* and thence to Mutual's *Behind the Screen* is astonishing. *The Rink*, the most balletic of all Chaplin's peformances, revealing the phenomenal skill on roller skates that was later to be seen in *Modern Times*, was evidently derived from the sketch Sydney had devised for Karno, *Skating*. A few films are more sophisticated and polished expositions of the Sennett principle of allowing a setting to inspire a series of comic improvisations – *The Floorwalker*, *The Fireman*, *The Adventurer*; but in others like *The Count* the comedy is rooted in a strong narrative-dramatic line.

With the beginning of 1917 however came an astonishing leap forward. *Easy Street*, *The Cure* and *The Immigrant*, which followed each other in the space of less than six months, launched the series of masterpieces that mark Chaplin's maturity. For *Easy Street* Chaplin erected a set which cost a sum unprecedented in comedy production, and which recreated a fantasy image of the London mean streets of his childhood. Eric Campbell plays the fearful Goliath who is king of Easy Street; Chaplin is the not overly-heroic David, the tyro cop who more than anything by luck brings peace to the street and turns Big Bad Bill into Sweet William. Chaplin's defeat of the impregnable heavy by the device of asphyxiating him with a handy street lamp (which the villain himself obligingly bends into position) is one of the best remembered of all comic images.

The Cure, in which Charlie is an incorrigible inebriate taking a cure at a spa, shows Chaplin's skill in comedy choreography at its most dextrous. *The Immigrant* is a potent mixture of pathos, irony and farce, its realism

The Pawnshop 1916.

only slightly belied by comic extravagance in the scenes aboard the immigrant ship. The supreme, ironic moment when a title 'Arrival in the Land of Liberty' is set against a shot of the newcomers from the Old World being corralled like cattle, remains as astonishing at each new viewing.

Chaplin, however, was still seeking greater independence for his creation. In July 1917 he signed a contract with First National Circuit, a combination of major theatre exhibitors, to produce eight pictures within sixteen months. Chaplin was to receive an advance of 125,000 dollars on each one, with an additional 15,000 dollars for each reel over the agreed length of two reels, and a bonus on signing of 75,000 dollars. It was believed to be the highest salary any man in any walk of life had ever received. The delivery period, however, was eventually to stretch from the foreseen sixteen months to almost five years, so completely had Chaplin embarked on the meticulous and unsparing methods of preparation and production that were to characterize the rest of his creative life.

The new contract gave Chaplin the possibility to create his own studio on the grounds of an old mansion, at the corner of La Brea and Sunset Boulevard. Here, behind the frontage nostalgically and fancifully designed to look like a row of English timbered cottages, all Chaplin's films up to *Limelight* were to be made. The building still stands – in recent years it was used by a record company – though the extensive lot behind has been built over.

The first two films under the First National contract continued the run of masterworks whose titles are still familiar even today. Both *A Dog's Life* and *Shoulder Arms*, following the lead of *The Immigrant*, made comedy out

The Chaplin Studios were designed to look like a row of English cottages – at least as seen by the American architects.

A Dog's Life *1918. Chaplin with Edna Purviance and Scraps.*

of notably grim areas of reality. In the first, Charlie's little ragamuffin is placed in a very real urban world, in which he battles with the other unemployed in the dole queue, and where his own mean existence is parallelled by that of his only friend, the stray dog Scraps.

Shoulder Arms was even more daring; and friends such as Douglas Fairbanks advised against attempting it. Made while the World War was still in progress, the unlikely sources of its humour were the mud and discomfort and hellish peril of the trenches of the Eastern front with Germany. Chaplin's instinct proved unerring. The men at the front, far from being offended to see their miseries thus metamorphosed into comedy were delighted; and more than half a century on this clown's eye view, this distorting mirror held to the nature of horror brings the reality of that far-off war much closer to modern spectators than many intense dramas of the day. *Shoulder Arms*, its flooded trenches, ravaged no-man's-land, hard ration biscuits and truculent spirit are remembered while the tragic dramas are forgotten.

Shoulder Arms *1918*. (*?*), *Park Jones, Charles Chaplin, Sydney Chaplin.*

Chaplin himself had volunteered for military service but had been rejected on medical grounds – which made all the more unjust the campaign waged by a minority in Britain and the States accusing him of being 'a slacker', charges which would be revived irrelevantly in the Cold War period of political paranoia and persecution. During 1918 Chaplin joined Douglas Fairbanks and Mary Pickford in national Liberty Bond-selling tours, and donated a short film, *The Bond* to the appeal.

His first post-war films, *Sunnyside* and *A Day's Pleasure* (which cast Chaplin as husband and father, much harassed by his efforts to give his family a day's outing) were necessarily an anti-climax. Chaplin had irritating domestic matters to distract him from his work: his marriage to Mildred Harris, who was sixteen at the time, had been precipitate and rapidly broke up, especially after the death of their first child, born deformed. The subsequent divorce proceedings were the first of the much publicised private problems which were recurrently to torment Chaplin.

No less remarkable than the rapidity of Chaplin's artistic development in these first phenomenally productive years of his career was the concurrent spread of his fame and popularity. An obscure English music hall artist in

1913, his name and face were known the world over by 1919 – long before the days of radio and television as publicity media.

With his first film, in January 1914, Chaplin was hailed by *Moving Picture Magazine* as 'a comedian of the first water'. Only two years later, the celebrated actress Minnie Maddern Fiske would contribute an article to *Harper's Weekly*, fearlessly entitled 'The Art of Charles Chaplin', and comparing him to Aristophanes, Plautus, Shakespeare, Rabelais and Fielding.

The public were there first, though; and even before the Keystone Studio had decided to name their new star on his films, had singled him out. Old men remember how as boys they called the nameless new comic (this was only in the very first weeks of 1914) by names they created for him: the trade press, too, invented a name for him, Edgar English. Once he was named, week after week the trade reviewers almost to a man praised the new Chaplin films. Sobel and Francis, in their *Chaplin. Genesis of a Clown*, point out that the enthusiasm was not entirely unanimous. As late as the spring of 1915 Sime Silverman, the redoubtable founder editor of *Variety*, called Chaplin's work 'mussy, messy and dirty': 'never anything dirtier was placed upon the screen than Chaplin's tramp'.

The public were not however to be deterred; and by 1915 Chaplin mania swept the English-speaking world. There were Chaplin sketches in every revue, Chaplin cartoons in every newspaper, Chaplin songs like 'The Charlie Chaplin Glide' or 'The Charlie Chaplin Walk', not to speak of the famous parody of 'Little Red Wing', 'The Moon Shines Bright on Charlie Chaplin'. There were Chaplin toys, Chaplin dolls, Chaplin comic books; and in 1915 Chaplin made his first appearance as a comic strip character in *The Funny Wonder*. In *Motion Picture Magazine* early in 1915 Charles J. McGuirk wrote of *Chaplinitis*:

'A little Englishman, quiet, unassuming, but surcharged with dynamite, is influencing the world right now. You can see him in the theater; you read of him in the magazines; you get a glimpse of his idiosyncracies in some twist of fashion. Among the happy youths of the slums, or the dandies of club-dom or college, an imitation of a Chaplin flirt of the coat, or the funny waddle of the comedian, is considered the last word in humour. To be Chaplinesque is to be funny; to waddle a few steps and then look naively at your audience, is a recognized form to which successful comedy is trending. You are artistic, perhaps. You were born with the gift of drawing or painting, or maybe you are a sculptor. Your gifts run to other lines. Maybe you are a poet or a writer. Very well; the thing to do now is to paint a portrait of Charles Chaplin in one of his characteristic poses, or to model him in clay. A poet can always sell a Chaplin poem; a writer finds a market for a Chaplin story. Any form of expressing Chaplin is what the public wants. The days of the minstrel's lay have come again. The world has Chaplin-itis.'

McGuirk contemplates the rarity of such an apparition, comparing the

Early cinema fame: the cover of Motion Picture Magazine *for July 1915.*

influence of Chaplin to that of Brummell or Andrew Jackson. 'Is it the man, or is it his work, or is his personality the embodiment of a world-thought?'

In the November 1915 issue of Royal Magazine, Langford Reed, an energetic Chaplin apologist, wrote: 'There are only two things which fill the public mind nowadays, the War and Charlie Chaplin, or, perhaps I should say, Charlie Chaplin and the War ...

'It is less than two years since he left for America, and his instantaneous rise to fame has quite overwhelmed his friends. Today Charlie Chaplin is one of the greatest living celebrities in the world, and he is justly regarded as a King of Mirth, his loyal subjects numbering many millions ...

'But his popularity in this country is nothing to his vogue in the United States, where there are Chaplin ties, Chaplin shirts, Chaplin cocktails, Chaplin yachts, and Chaplin clubs and societies. One American city has a street named after him'.

What is most striking about Chaplin's first reviews is that practically from the start writers took him *seriously*. No-one wrote in this way about Fatty Arbuckle, Ford Sterling or even John Bunny; or, for many years, about Buster Keaton. But from the beginning, even in the wholly practical-minded pages of the trade magazines, Chaplin was considered in terms appropriate to substantial works of art. In *The Moving Picture World*, aimed at exhibitors and film bookers, Louis Reeves Harrison wrote of *His Trysting Place*, in October 1914: 'Productions of obvious merit need no publicity. They take care of themselves, whatever critics, either favourable or carping, may say. Their commercial value lies in their inherent opposition of good structure, better treatment and the best of acting. The comic spirit is entirely too deep and subtle for me to define. It defies analysis. The human aspect is certainly dominant. It is funniest when it is rich in defects of character. The incongruity of Chaplin's portrayals, his extreme seriousness, his sober attention to trivialities, his constant errors, and as constant resentment of what happens to him, all this has to be seen to be enjoyed ...

'While learned gentlemen are discussing Oedipus and attempting to explain the extremely simple plot of Shakespeare's *Comedy of Errors*, the reduplication of a coincidence, we are having more than one veritable *Comedy of Errors* in real life, before our very eyes, so why go so far afield? The Keystone comedies are delightfully realistic ...'

Within two years of Chaplin's arrival in pictures, writers in the most serious magazine had no inhibitions about writing about his 'art'. The article by Mrs Fiske has already been noted. In February 1917 Harvey O'Higgins, a well-known playwright later to become a screenwriter, contributed an article on 'Charlie Chaplin's Art' to *The New Republic*. After instancing the miracles that Chaplin can perform with his walking stick he urges, 'do not believe that such acting is a matter of crude and simple means. It is as subtle in its naturalism as the shades of intonation in a really tragic speech. In one of Chaplin's films, another actor, disguised as Chaplin, walked into the pictures and was received by the audience with a preliminary titter of welcome.

He went though a number of typical Chaplin antics with a drinking fountain that squirted water in his face. There was half-hearted laughter. He was not funny. He moved through a succession of comic 'stunts' unsuccessfully before it dawned on me that this was not Chaplin at all. When Chaplin followed in, and repeated the exact passages that had failed, the laughter was enormous. It was the difference between a man acting a comic scene and man living it, and the difference was apparent in a thousand niceties of carriage and gesture and expression of face. In this hairbreadth of difference lies the triumph of Chaplin's art ...'

O'Higgins concludes: 'There is no doubt, as Mrs Fiske has said, that he is a great artist. And he is a great lesson and encouragement to anyone who loves an art or practices it, for he is an example of how the best can be the most successful, and of how a real talent can triumph over the most appalling limitations put upon its expression, and of how the popular eye can recognize such a talent without the aid of the pundits of culture and even in spite of their anathema.'

Stanley Kauffmann, commenting on this particular article by O'Higgins (*American Film Criticism*, 1972), has said that the rapid promotion of Chaplin's work to the subject of serious discussion was largely due 'of course to his quality; some of it was due to opportune timing. He came along just as cultural attitudes towards the film began to change'. His work and personality contributed largely to effecting these changes.

In more recent years – notably since the period of the most acute American political hostility towards Chaplin – many writers have become frankly embarrassed by the extreme adulation of these early years. Sobel and Francis attempt to rationalize, in terms of 1977, the feelings and enthusiasms of writers of 1917:

'Nevertheless it is possible to say that after his initial success among those who saw him only as a hilarious comedian, many highly intelligent people were not prepared to forgo the pleasure of seeing him – people who otherwise might never have given a thought to slapstick comedy. Perhaps it was his grace of movement, the beauty of his gestures, the brilliance of his miming which encouraged them to consider him in other terms. There is something vastly satisfying, after all, in the sight of even the humblest of craftsmen who is master of his craft. One is tempted to read deeper and more significant meanings into it, especially if the tendency of the age is to feel threatened by a devouring industrialization which seems bent on crushing the individual craftsman – a mood characteristic of the early years of this century.

'Then, again, it is difficult for thinking people to stop thinking. An intellectual who enjoyed Chaplin found it as impossible to accept him at the comedian's own level as it would be for Prince Charming to keep Cinderella dressed as a scullery maid. And therein lay the intellectual's dilemma: how was he to reconcile his disdain for slapstick with his very real delight at one of its masters? The problem was never solved satisfactorily. Serious critics betrayed a painful inner conflict; between admiration and shame, between hostility and uncertainty. How they wrote about Chaplin was largely determined by how they tried to deal with those conflicts ...'

Returning, however, to the actual period of these writings, an article of December 1920 by Herbert Howe of *Picture-Play* reveals the uneasiness of fans and critics at the thought that Chaplin was changing and that this change explained the unprecedented delay between the release of Chaplin pictures. The article is called 'What's the Matter With Chaplin?': 'It seems to be the fashion just now to take a furtive boot at Charlie Chaplin where he is most sensitive. Slapstick artists of the press have been banging him about the ears with the hot-air bladder. Their evangelical purpose is to chastise him for his sins of omission and to remind him that this is no time to be doing a Rip Van Winkle. They haven't had a good laugh for a long time despite their loud guffaws at the antics of other pantaloons, who now and then they covertly suggest are giving Chaplin the dust.

'Chaplin is being put to the inquisition because he has failed in his duty as court jester to the world. We must admit that the hand that wields the slapstick rocks the world. And no-one rocks it more merrily on its axis than Charlie ...'

Mr Howe, attributed Chaplin's apparent inactivity, perhaps with some justice, though in fact he was, of course, laboriously preparing *The Kid* at the time, to the domestic problems posed by the break-up of the marriage with Mildred Harris: 'It must cramp an artist's style to be wed to one not a muse. Although, Heaven knows, matrimony doesn't have time to cramp most movie stars. Chaplin, unfortunately, is sensitive. He never knew when he might return home to find that Madame Chaplin during his absence had hung the family skeleton on the clothes-line. Madame had an annoying penchant for airing the family linen before the public.'

One section of Howe's article – written at the peak of Chaplin's popularity – is peculiarly fascinating, given the hindsight of the troubles which Chaplin was to experience with American opinion a quarter of a century later. 'Of late,' he says, 'Charlie has been the victim of much ill rumour – a rather hapless victim because he seems constitutionally unsuited to verbal combat. The most criminal accusation hurled at him seems to be "tightwad". In contrast to most of the movie plutocrats, Charlie is a Silas Marner. To think that a movie star possesses only one automobile and one chauffeur. It's heinous! And I don't think he has a valet. At least he has never talked of one, and I've never seen any one in livery hanging about him. His automobile is just a cheap six or seven thousand dollar stock car. It hasn't any gilt on it, no kalogram, or aluminium, or anything worth while. He likes simple food and eats it. He dresses most simply.

'Perhaps this quiet manner of living is the reason he has been accused of bolshevist and socialist sympathies. Most people using those terms don't know what they mean, anyhow, so it doesn't matter. I do not know that it is an offence to be a socialist, now that things are settling down again. This is presumably a free country, where one may elect his own political party or religion. As for Charlie being a Socialist, a Republican, a Democrat – he's an actor. He may take a casual interest in politics, just as he does in art, music, and the Vernon boxing matches. These issues are in the minority. His work holds the overwhelming majority. The public does not pay to see the man Chaplin, it pays to see the artist, and we only protest when the artist's goods deteriorate and fall off as Chaplin's have of late.

'A mind divided cannot accomplish its best. Chaplin has had various vitiating claims upon his mind. We hope he soon may be freed of them.'

The First Critic

It seemed appropriate that the first serious monograph on a film artist in the history of cinema criticism, should be devoted to Charles Chaplin. It seemed appropriate too that it should be written by the greatest pioneer of film criticism.

Louis Delluc's career as *cinéaste* lasted barely a decade; but it was instrumental in forming an attitude and a climate which made possible the classical French cinema of Renoir and Clair. Delluc was born in Cadouin in the Dordogne on 14th October 1890. At fifteen he arrived in Paris, instantly made his way into the artistic world and commenced a precocious career as poet and journalist, contributing theatre criticism to *Comoedia illustrée*. Until 1914 he appears to have held the cinema in the snobbish scorn frequent in people of the theatre, though he did confess an admiration for Louis Lumière and Max Linder among the French artists of the pre-war years. Delluc's conversion came however in this year when he first saw De Mille's *The Squaw Man* and the early Chaplin Keystone shorts.

From this point was born a feverish and unflagging enthusiasm, out of which Delluc developed his theory of cinema as an art in its own right, with its own aesthetic rules. Despite the interruptions of the First World War, Delluc began to write prolifically; and in 1917 established his own first magazine *Film*, in collaboration with Henri Diamant-Berger. Their contributors included from time to time Colette, Cocteau, André Antoine, Aragon and Guillaume Apollinaire. The following year Delluc secured a daily film column in *Paris Midi* which under the rubric 'Cinema et Cie' introduced the newspaper public for the first time to real creative criticism: until that time film columnists had contented themselves with being the willing publicists of the distributors and exhibitors.

Delluc next established a new weekly, *Ciné-Club*, which shortly afterwards changed its name to *Cinéa*. At the masthead it carried the slogan which was to be central to Delluc's effort during the years still spared to him: 'The French cinema must be *cinema*: the French cinema must be *French*'. Delluc carried his principles into practice. He abhorred above all the practice of literary adaptation, and so wrote his own scenarios to exemplify the autonomous creation of cinematic works. The first of these scenarios, *La Fête Espagnole* was directed by Germaine Dulac; in 1920 Delluc himself directed the first of the first of the half dozen films he was to realize, most of which starred his wife, Eve Francis. It was whilst making the last of these that Delluc, whose lungs had suffered grave damage during the war, fell fatally ill. He died in Paris on 22nd March 1924.

Delluc and his followers – as well as Germaine Dulac they were Abel Gance, Marcel L'Herbier and Jean Epstein – were styled the 'Impressionist School'. In their aim of founding a new national tradition, they looked for inspiration to the cinemas of other countries. In 1920 Delluc and his friends established the world's first film society, which was instrumental in popularising the work of the Swedish school and of the then new German Expressionist cinema.

Above all, however, they found their most admired masters in the United States: the delayed release in France of D. W. Griffith's *Birth of a Nation*, *Intolerance* and *Broken Blossoms* as well as the expansive Westerns of Thomas Ince provided a thrilling shock. But above all there was Chaplin; and in 1921 Delluc paid his tribute with *Charlot* (published in Paris by Maurice de Brunoff. An English translation by Hamish Miles was offered to a somewhat bemused English public by John Lane the Bodley Head the following year).

The book was a work of propaganda as well as of loving appreciation. Chaplin and his works were the ideal example to prove Delluc's theory of cinema as an autonomous art. First, and most contentious though, was the claim that the cinema was an art at all. A decade earlier Ricciotto Canudo, a predecessor and inspiration of Delluc as an aesthetician of the cinema, had named the film 'the seventh art', an amalgam, as he demonstrated, of its six older sisters. But in the twenties it was even harder to convince the unconverted than it is today, more than sixty years later. Delluc opened his book with a magnificently challenging 'Prelude': 'To the creative artist of the cinema, the mask of Charlie Chaplin has just the same importance as the traditional mask of Beethoven has to the musical composer.

'I hope that this pronouncement will automatically eliminate all superfluous readers, and that we shall only be concerned with people who are capable of understanding each other.

'That sets our minds at rest. And now we can go on.'

Going on, Delluc's aggressive method continues in the same course of drawing comparisons, without apology, between Chaplin and the highest representatives of their art in other fields. Section II, following the 'Prelude' is on 'The Mask': 'Some have been pleased to find there a family resemblance to the finest heads of the Japanese stylists: others prefer to recall for it some of the magnificently learned expressions of Velasquez, some bold, bare faces of Albert Durer, or something of the precise outline of the Flemish primitives. And, in intention at least, this is not absurd: at bottom it is right. For what does strike us in the latest presentation of this mask is how clearly it has taken on the quality of a painter's work. A living pictorial art! We have come very near to realizing that. Already there is one portrait in the gallery.'

For his own part, Delluc prefers to find a Latin quality in the mask – not the 'profound dryness, that sour reserve or that composed disorder' of the old masters of the north and east of France, but rather something from the court portrait painters from Jean de Paris down to Clouet – 'those faces come in procession, shaven and subtle, ironic, sentimentally sensual, acute and unheeding; there is wit gnawing at their muscles, easing the treacherous tightness of the nerves, and in their eyes flits an unfathomed life.'

Delluc's purpose here is not just a snobbish recital of art history connaissance. He cites these distinguished and vivid examples to jolt the reader into a new attitude from which he may see afresh the screen portrait of Chaplin; thereafter he abandons the whole notion of comparisons. For what, he now asks, is the good of seeking an author for the portrait. For Charlie is unique as the artist and the work of art at one and the same time. Chaplin, he says, pursuing his own central theory of cinema, has accomplished something which is possible only in the cinema, 'to pattern and model and sculpt one's own body, one's own features, to make a transposition of art ... And that is why, in this art of the living picture, this man is the first full-fledged creator. And so far he remains the only one'.

*   *   *

In the third section of his book, which he entitles 'The Pioneer', Delluc explores with quite remarkable insights an aspect of Chaplin's work which had by that time struck comparatively few of his contemporaries – the darker side and essential tragedy of most of his comedy. Returning to his original plan Delluc again cites the best names for comparison: Molière (who became 'mighty tedious, as Chaplin never will'), and Nijinski.

Nijinski and Chaplin are, he says, alike inventors in their art; but again he ranks Chaplin higher. 'Nijinski, the representative figure of our epoch, stands for only one epoch of the dance in all the history of the dance. But Charlie is the pioneer of the very first epoch of his art, and he is in some measure responsible for the plaything having become an art ... Chaplin interprets himself. And he sums up, not what is being done, like Nijinski, but what is going to be done.'

Nijinski, he says was consumed with the flame of creation. 'They say he is mad now. Hail and farewell!' He sees, he says, such immense sadness in Chaplin that the man will be lucky if he does not die in a madhouse. In *A Dog's Life*, then one of Chaplin's newest films, 'He is hungry, hungry with all his being. He will never be able to eat again'. Far more tragic, though, in Delluc's eyes, was *Shoulder Arms*, which had been attacked on its first appearance in some quarters as being in bad taste in making comedy out of the recent and bloody war. 'The war through Chaplin's eyes ... An hour of laughter if you like – but say, rather, an hour of lashes, one after the

A Dog's Life *1918. Chaplin with Scraps.*

other ... When dogs are wretched they bay at the moon. That war film of Chaplin bays most terribly at the moon.'

Delluc goes on to analyse Chaplin's career and the formative influences on his comedy development. Chaplin's best school, he concludes, was the Karno pantomime troupes. Characteristically dragging in an allusion to Agamemnon and Electra, he is full of admiration for the English music hall comedy, endlessly working away at the same imagery of bicycle thieves, billiard players, drunks returning home, boxing lessons, failed conjurors and frustrated sopranos, but always with a distinct and highly polished sense of rhythm and structure. Chaplin, in his four or five years with Karno, 'worked at getting the feel of this repertory with its neat and suggestive technique. It was to come in useful for him later, in the cinema ...'

In his very perceptive assessment of Chaplin's influence upon American film comedy, Delluc reveals his distaste for the old pre-war primitives which were, he says 'made up – and there are still lots of them – of very stupid slapstick'. Chaplin, in contrast, had learned from Karno the value of expression and that 'fling your limbs in no matter how joyous a frenzy, it comes to nothing unless you can get the movements – or the lack of movements – of the mask' – in other words, comic action has to develop out of character. Justifiably Delluc attributes to Chaplin's immediate influence a new and heightened sense of character comedy in American slapstick comedy, and the marked development of Mack Sennett's talents as a producer. (Delluc greatly admired *Mickey*, a full-length comedy designed to exhibit the outstanding talent of Sennett's adored star Mabel Normand).

A section of Delluc's book which is still as valuable and illuminating today as when it first appeared is his chapter on Chaplin's method. Even at that stage of his career, Chaplin liked to work in secret and behind closed doors; but Delluc assembles three descriptions of Chaplin at work which are still the most valuable testimonies we have. One is Max Linder's record of his meetings with Chaplin, published in *Le Film* in 1919, and which will be discussed in a later chapter. Linder, who was particularly admired as a one-take artist, was deeply impressed by the systematic and painstaking methods at the Chaplin lot, and astounded that Chaplin would shoot 36,000 feet of film for a picture that ended up as 1,800 feet.

The second account of Chaplin at work was by an employee, Elsie Codd, whose article had been syndicated in magazines throughout the world in early 1920. Miss Codd revealed how Chaplin had used his growing independence to expend more time and money on his productions; how he worked without a script; and how his ideas very frequently grew out of a single comic incident he had witnessed.

An even more significant treasure which Delluc enshrined in his little book, however, was one of the most comprehensive accounts Chaplin ever vouchsafed of his views on comedy. Delluc retrieved it from an article published in 1918 in *American Magazine*, entitled *What People Laugh At*. 'You won't blame me,' apologises Delluc, 'for saying so much about the technical cares of a creative comedian ... Chaplin himself says it more simply, or else with more love.'

'Whenever I meet people who ask me to tell them the secret of making this world of mine laugh,' says Chaplin; 'I feel ill at ease, and I generally try to slip away unobserved. There is nothing more mysterious about my comicality on the screen than there is about Harry Lauder's way of getting his public to laugh. You'll find that both of us know a few simple truths about human nature, and we make use of them in our jobs. And when all is said and done, the foundation of all success is only a knowledge of human nature, whether you're a tradesman, or an innkeeper, a publisher or an actor.

'Now, for example, what I rely on more than anything else is bringing the public before someone who is in a ridiculous and embarrassing position.

'Thus, the mere fact of a hat being blown away isn't funny in itself. What is, is to see its owner running after it, with his hair blown about and his coat-tails flying. A man is walking along the street – that doesn't lend itself to laughter. But placed in a ridiculous and embarrassing position the human being becomes a cause of laughter to his fellow-creatures. Every comic situation is based on that. And comic films had immediate success because most of them showed policemen falling down drain-holes, stumbling into white-wash pails, falling out of carts and put to all kinds of botheration. Here are people who stand for the dignity of power, and often deeply imbued with this idea, being made ridiculous and getting laughed at, and the sight of *their* mishaps makes the public want to laugh twice as much as if it were only ordinary citizens undergoing the same transformations.'

'And still funnier is the person in a ludicrous position who, in spite of it, refuses to admit that anything out of the ordinary is happening, and is obstinate in preserving his dignity. The best example is given by the drunken man who, though given away by his speech and his walk, wants to convince us that he has not touched a drop. He is much funnier than the frankly merry gentleman who shows his drunkenness as plain as day and laughs because you see it. Drunkenness on the stage is generally slight with a touch of dignity, because producers have learnt that this pretence is funny in itself.

'That is why all my films rest on the idea of getting myself into awkward situations, so as to give me the chance of being desperately serious in my attempts to look like a very normal little gentleman. That is why my chief concern, no matter how painful the position I get myself into, is always to pick up my little cane at once, and put my bowler hat straight, and adjust my necktie – even after I've just fallen on my head. I am so sure of this that I do not try only to get myself into these embarrassing positions, but I count on putting others also into them.

'When I work on this principle I make every effort to economise my means. I mean by this that when one single happening can by itself arouse two separate bursts of laughter, it's better than two separate happenings doing so. In *The Adventurer* I succeeded in placing myself on a balcony where I have to eat an ice with a young lady. On the floor beneath I place a stout, respectable, well-dressed lady, sitting at a table. Then, while eating my ice, I let fall a spoonful which slides down my trousers, and then falls from the balcony down the lady's neck. The first laugh is caused by my own em-barrassment, the second, and much the greater, comes from the arrival of the ice on the lady's neck, and she screams and dances about. One single action has been enough, but it has made two people ridiculous and set laughter free twice.'

Chaplin goes on to explain that this particular gag sheds light on two traits of human nature. One is the pleasure in seeing 'richness and luxury in distress'; the other is the tendency to share the emotions of the personage on the stage or screen. To illustrate the first point, he explains that if he had made the ice fall down the neck of a poor housewife, the result would have been to excite sympathy rather than laughter. 'To let an ice fall down a rich woman's neck is, in the public's opinion, to let her have just what she deserves.' It implies a somewhat cruel type of humour; but here Chaplin understood the public of 1918.

Louis Delluc, whose book Charlot *was the first serious study of any cinema actor.*

As to the matter of sympathy, he explains that the audience shivers with the ice-cream victim; and has sufficient experience of its own embarrassments to be able to share that of the actor. 'If one used something which the public does not at once recognize, the effect would be partly lost. On this was based all the throwing about of cream tarts and the like in the early films. Everyone knows how easily these tarts are squashed, and so everyone can appreciate the feelings of the actor who gets one thrown at him'.

He is often asked, he says, where he gets the idea of his particular character. He says it is a blend of many English types he saw in his London days. When he left the Karno company, he was uncertain what his new comic character should be. 'But after a little I thought of all those little Englishman I had seen with their little black moustaches, their tight clothes and their bamboo canes, and I fixed on these as my model.' The cane, he felt was his best find: it had rapidly become a trade mark to make him known, and he had elaborated its uses until it had acquired a comic character of its own. 'I don't think I quite knew at first how true it is that, for millions of individuals, a walking-stick marks a man as rather a "swell". And so when I come shuffling on to the scene with my little cane and my serious air, I give the impression of an attempt at dignity, and that is exactly my object.'

He attributes his virtually overnight success in pictures at the early age of twenty-one partly to the fact that he was then a seasoned pro of seven years' experience; but also in large degree to the example of his mother who 'was' – the use of the past tense is interesting – 'the most astounding mimic I ever saw'. He describes how, when he was a child, his mother would stay for hours at the window, observing what went on in the street, impersonating people's actions, interpreting from them their feelings and their biographies. This, says her son, taught him the importance of observation.

It was an observation which he had carried over to practical professional use outside the immediate business of creating character. 'When I am watching one of my own films at a public performance, I keep one eye on the screen and the other and my two ears on the spectators. I notice what makes them laugh and what does not. If, for example, at several performances, the public does not laugh at some touch which I meant to be funny, I at once set to work to find what was wrong with the idea or its execution, or perhaps with the process of photographing it. And very often I notice a little laugh for some gesture which was not studied, and then I prick up my ears and try to find out why this particular point has made them laugh. In a way, when I go to see one of my films, I am like a tradesman watching what his customers are carrying out or buying or doing.'

He describes how observation has given him the idea for his films. Watching firemen answering a call led him to picture himself in their situation, and to *The Fireman*. Likewise an escalator in a big store suggested *The Floorwalker*; a boxing match, *Champion Charlie* (*The Champion*), a labour exchange, *A Dog's Life*. A bit of business which he introduced into *The Cure* and which was to remain a favourite gag was suggested by his embarrassment in a restaurant when he thought a fellow-diner was greeting him amiably, only to discover that the man was signalling flirtatiously to a pretty girl sitting behind.

He goes on to consider the importance of contrast and surprise, always contriving to have himself chased by a cop or other heavy whose lumbering bulk contrasts with his own diminutive size and agility. 'Everyone knows that the persecuted little individual always has the sympathy of the crowd. Knowing this liking for the weakest, I contrive to emphasize my weakness by working my shoulders, and assuming a pitiable expression, and taking on a frightened air. All that, of course, is the art of pantomime; but if I were a little bigger I should have more trouble in winning sympathy, for I should then have been deemed capable of looking after myself. But as I am, the public, even while laughing at my appearance, really feels for me.' As an example of his use of contrast he illustrates the end of *A Dog's Life* in which, wishing to show himself painstakingly planting up his field, one seed at a time in holes poked with his forefinger, he chose the largest field he could find to achieve the maximum absurdity.

He discusses the importance of surprise: 'I force myself to make my personal gestures come in some surprising form.' He instances the scene in *The Immigrant* in which he is seen from behind, and the convulsive movements of his shoulders suggest that he is in the throes of seasickness. When he finally turns round we discover that he has merely been wrestling with a fish on his line.

He goes on to discuss the dangers of being too funny, of exhausting the audience with non-stop laughter. He prefers to scatter the laughter: 'Two or three bursts of laughter are better than a continuous bubbling of amusement or the explosion of your audience for several minutes.' He speaks of the great labour involved in making a film – how he will sometimes shoot twenty hours of film to get his twenty minutes – and of the danger of trusting other judgements than one's own. He speaks of the need for restraint in every aspect of the work: 'One reason why I dislike my early films is that restraint was difficult in them.'

'Perhaps,' he concludes, 'I have not always succeeded owing to my methods, but I do prefer a thousand times to get a laugh by an intelligent act than by anything brutal or banal. There is no mystery in making the public laugh. My whole secret is in keeping my eyes open and my wits wide-awake for everything capable of being used in my films. I have studied human nature because, without knowledge of it, I should have done nothing in my calling. And, as I said before, a knowledge of mankind is at the bottom of all success.'

(In the first chapter of this book attention was drawn to Chaplin's very distinctive literary style. That style is certainly not apparent in the article from which the foregoing quotations are taken: and the practised journalist will instantly recognise the phrasing and tones of an article concocted by the interview method. It was most probably the work of Rob Wagner, a classical scholar who was Chaplin's favoured literary assistant at this time.

On the other hand the film references are so precise and the opinions so authoritative as to suggest that this is a very accurate record of Chaplin's view of his art and craft after four years' unremitting labour at the movies.)

Delluc, rejoicing in the way that Chaplin's work vindicated his own view of cinema as an independent and autonomous art form with its own singular expressive means, concluded his essay with enraptured, impressionistic descriptions of the individual films. He preceded it with his summation of Chaplin's importance, a passage which was to prove prophetic:

'Charlie Chaplin's talent is governed by strict method. It is his own method, and consummate in its art and precision. But this method is itself founded on another one, and the starting-point is the science – or the tradition – of the Humpsti-Bumpsties. These music-hall oddities have always been a joy to Paris, a pair of opposites who go through their manoeuvres with harmony, and with a mathematical precision as grave as that of the French tragic authors of the seventeenth century. Their madness has both observation and paradox in it. It is a highly flavoured concoction which seems to do violence to your attention, smacks truth in the face, and forces laughter. Sometimes there is only one person on the stage, and then the raciness of the school is felt best. Who can forget Little Tich?

'Hardly a week passes but a real variety show gives us the sight of one of these *baroque*, disciplined performances. In 1914 all the town flocked to see the man – I forget his name – who played a bicycle thief, and he was a humorist on the grand scale. Recently Sam Barton appeared in an identical one-man act, and Grock is the delight of all Parisians.

'Charlie Chaplin is head and shoulders above all that. Above, because he will go farther than the others, and won't work all his life long on one single theme of buffoonery. Remembering the development of Max Dearly's talent, one sees what can be expected from Chaplin. If he has time to do all that he has in him to do, this admirable ironist will have an exceptional place in the history of entertainment.'

Self-Portrait: II

Self-Portrait – II

In 1921 Chaplin enjoyed his greatest success so far with *The Kid*; and followed it with *The Idle Class*, in which he played a dual role as a bibulous and eccentric aristocrat and the little tramp, the gentleman's double, who turns up at a fancy dress ball and is mistaken by the wife and family for the aristocrat himself. He had just commenced work on a new two-reeler *Pay Day* when the cumulative effects of seven years' non-stop work and the disagreeable divorce case with his first wife caught up with him. He failed to arrive at the studio for the second day's work on *Pay Day*, and instead booked a passage to Europe. At the Los Angeles railway station he was seen off by Edna Purviance and other members of the company, and his brother Sydney, whose parting injunction to Carl Robinson, his press secretary who was to accompany him on the trip, was 'For God's sake don't let him get married'. From New York he was seen off by Douglas Fairbanks and Mary Pickford, who at this time were among his closest Hollywood friends.

The trip was the occasion for an international celebration of idolatry which can be seen as the very peak of Chaplin's phenomenal popularity. Fortunately he recorded every stage of the triumphal progress through Europe and his own reaction to it, the mixture of amazement, gratification and awe at the deference of the great and the adoration of the multitude. On his return he engaged a newspaperman, Monta Bell, to set down his experiences and impressions. Bell was later to become an assistant to Chaplin on *A Woman of Paris*, and in time became a director in his own right. Bell has often been credited as a literary ghost; but the book – it was published in the United States as *My Trip Abroad* and in Britain as *My Wonderful Visit* – is so close in vocabulary and style to other Chaplin writings (notably, of course, *My Autobiography*) that it seems a reasonable assumption that Bell acted only as a loyal stenographer and sub-editor in recording Chaplin's own direct impressions.

My Trip Abroad consists of around fifty thousand words; and is written in the present tense, with a slightly staccato impressionism characteristic of the period. The publicity for the English edition declared, 'This is not a book written *about* Charlie Chaplin by someone else. *It is written by himself*, and it tells you of his early life and of some of his doings in America; but it deals more especially with his experiences in London, sets down his impressions of all he sees and hears, and gives his comments, so that in the end the reader gains a real insight into Charlie's character and feels that he knows the man. Everyone who has enjoyed the Chaplin impersonations on the film will want this book to discover the real man behind them'.

Chaplin headed his first chapter 'I Decide to Play Hookey'; and explained that he was stirred to the search for 'an emotional holiday' by three factors: a bout of influenza that had made him recognize his exhaustion and had faced him with the spectre of a possible nervous breakdown; the nostalgia surrounding a steak and kidney pie at the home of Montague Glass, the author of the best-selling *Potash and Perlmutter*; and a telegram telling him that *The Kid* was about to open in London. He took stock that he had never attended the first showing of one of his pictures. 'I had been missing something vital and stimulating. I had success, but it was stored away somewhere. I had never opened the package and tasted it. I sort of wanted to be patted on the back.' Perhaps, he speculated darkly, *The Kid* might be his last picture, so that there would never be another chance to bask in the spotlight. Europe was new: 'I wanted to see Europe – England, France, Germany and Russia.'

First, though, he saw Chicago and New York and had a fore-taste of the mobs that were to remain in attendance throughout the European progress. At first, he admitted, he actually liked the crowds and their enthusiasm; and was able to transform what he called his 'prop' smile into an expression of real pleasure. He found it harder to enjoy the reporters, who regularly asked the same questions: what did he do with his old moustaches; did he want to play Hamlet; was he going to marry again; and (most ominously) was he a Bolshevik?

In New York he was inveigled into attending the premières of Pickford's *Little Lord Fauntleroy* and Fairbanks' *The Three Musketeers*. The presence at each of these events of all three of the nation's idols was the occasion for unprecedented crowd hysteria; and at the showing of *The Three Musketeers* Chaplin came off rather badly. Swept away by the sea of people, he was repeatedly punched and pushed by policemen who could not be convinced that he was Charlie Chaplin – not surprisingly perhaps since fans had snatched his tie, half his collar and a fragment neatly cut from the seat of his trousers by a woman with a pair of scissors, as souvenirs. By the time he joined the stars in their box he had also lost the buttons from his waist-coat, had his shirt pulled out and his face somewhat scratched. He sensed severe disapproval from his friends, who had arrived unscathed, though he congratulated himself on having behaved admirably, even sustaining the 'prop' smile through all these manifestations of fan fever which, in 1921, was still a comparatively new phenomenon.

There were other discoveries to be made in New York. Chaplin's friend Max Eastman, a writer of marked radical views, took him to a left-wing party, where he was profoundly impressed and moved by an encounter with an International Workers of The World activist about to return to an eighteen-year gaol sentence; but still with 'a light in his eyes that I have never seen before, a light that must have shone from his soul'.

Chaplin also gave a dinner party of his own, at which the guests, apart, inevitably, from Fairbanks and Pickford, included the playwright Edward Knoblock, Heywood Broun, Alexander Woollcott, Eastman and Madame Maurice Maeterlinck. The description of the party is a fascinating glimpse of the social life of young intelligentsia of the twenties: they played charades; and Chaplin and Madame Maeterlinck performed a parody of the death scene from *La Dame aux Caméllias*, with Marguerite's cough proving so infectious that Armand succumbs ahead of the heroine.

Chaplin's return to England was strikingly different from his departure, steerage class, eight years earlier as a member of the Karno pantomime troupe. 'There is nothing like money,' he reflected frankly; 'It does make life so easy.' He found however that his fame made life on shipboard as uncomfortable in its way as his battles with the première crowds in New York. Whether he went to the gymnasium or the Turkish baths or to any other part of the ship, he found himself surrounded by curious crowds, demanding autographs, asking questions, offering undesired advice. For a few pleasurable moments he embarked on a game of cricket with the stokers (one of whom turned out to be a failed actor with whom he had once worked); but quickly found that the first-class passengers had turned out to stare. The 'prop' smile clearly wore thinnest with the professional photographers. When leaving New York Chaplin adamantly refused to adopt valedictory poses in front of the Statue of Liberty. Later he was forced to take strong measures with a cameraman who announced that he had embarked on the journey with the specific assignment of filming Chaplin *en route* for England. His most disagreeable experience was to be insulted by a passenger who had got up an amateur concert on board, and was affronted because Chaplin, not unreasonably, would not expose himself by appearing in it. 'Never mind,' he told the rest of the audience; 'You can see Charlie Chaplin any time for a nickel.'

Chaplin related how his nervousness and excitement grew as the ship approached England. At Cherbourg the vessel was overrun by a boatload of journalists and photographers. At Southampton there was to be a civic reception, with a speech of welcome by the Mayor. Chaplin actually confessed disappointment that the crowd was not bigger than it turned out to be.

His frankness about the feelings that overcame him is very winning; and certainly could hardly have been the work of a literary 'ghost'. Among the old acquaintances who met him at Southampton and accompanied him to London was his cousin Aubrey Chaplin, a publican. 'He has not seen me in ten years,' Chaplin confided; 'I sort of want to pose before him a little. I want to shock him; no, not exactly to shock him, but surprise him. I find myself deliberately posing and just for him. I want to be different, and I

Shoulder Arms *1918. Edna Purviance, Charles Chaplin, Sydney Chaplin.*

want him to know that I am a different person ...' Chaplin's self-portrait in this way gives a fascinating revelation of the actor's rapid and continuing readjustment to the circumstances of his idolatry – an idolatry which he had remained for a large part unaware whilst remaining in California, immersed in his work.

All London seemed to be in the grip of a Chaplin fever. The comedian had to be manhandled by police through the crowds at Waterloo. He was thrust into his car to find that he had lost his cousin and the rest of his escort, but was in company with a bewildered and bleeding man who had also been thrown into the car by the police who believed him to be one of Chaplin's official companions. With difficulty he was delivered to the Ritz, where he was compelled to make appearances on the balcony of his suite – though the police requested him to desist from throwing down roses for fear of injury to the people struggling to retrieve them in the street below. Again Chaplin's reactions to the fervour are fascinating. He was unashamedly thrilled and delighted; but reflected, 'thinking over what I have done, it has not been very much. Nothing to call forth all this. *Shoulder Arms* was pretty good, perhaps, but all this clamour over a moving-picture actor!' 'If I could only do something – solve the unemployment problem or make some grand gesture – in answer to all this'; and again, 'I feel like doing something big. What an opportunity for a politician to say something and do something big! I never felt such affection'.

It is in *My Trip Abroad* that Chaplin first described the powerful nostalgia for the scenes and events and people of his childhood that seems never entirely to have left him. It would be reasonable to expect that a successful man would struggle to reject the memories of a youth that contained so much privation and misfortune. Chaplin, perhaps, remained acutely aware how much of his creative gift was rooted in that youth, and was determined to keep his hold upon it. 'I want,' he wrote 'to commune with myself and the years that are gone.' In 1921 he could still find many souvenirs of those years: an old blind vagrant under Westminster Bridge; a girl who had been a skivvy in one of the houses where he had lived, and whom he met with the illegitimate child which had been the cause of her dismissal. He even claimed to recognize the tub outside one house, where as a boy he had washed in the mornings. His nostalgia evidently lent a romantic colouring to all he saw: 'How lovely the cockneys are! How romantic the figures, how sad, how fascinating! Their lovely eyes. How patient they are! Nothing conscious about them. No affectation, their beautifully gay selves, serene in their limitations, perfect in their type.' 'God,' he wrote a little further on, 'if I could only do something for all of them!

'But there are too many – too many. Good impulses so often die before this "too many".'

He was touched by the natural courtesy of the people of Kennington when they recognized him. Despite their curiosity they followed him at a respectful distance so as not to disturb him; and only when he acknowledged them did they press around with their good wishes. The romantic nostalgia was an ambivalent feeling, nevertheless; and he confessed that a dinner party that night at the Ritz, with Edward Knoblock and other friends, 'did much to lift me from the depression into which the afternoon in Kennington had put me'.

Interestingly, at this dinner party, Knoblock suggested that this was the peak of Chaplin's career. 'I am inclined to agree with him,' said Chaplin, who thereupon played a bizarre practical joke on one of his friends, who had suggested that this would be the perfect time for him to die, by staging his own death and resurrection.

My Trip Abroad – and perhaps after all the English title, *My Wonderful Visit* is finally more appropriate – seems to be at once a chronicle of this period that symbolized the apogee of Chaplin's career and popularity; and the record of an experiment in reconciling past and future. When Chaplin next explored London, to rediscover the old human landmarks from his youth – a hoarse and bottle-nosed old tomato vendor, a coffee-stall, the prostitutes of Piccadilly – it was in the company of his smart friends; and from Kennington and Newington Butts, the party deviated to Park Lane to call on George Fitzmaurice the American director, who was then living there. Chaplin recalled that there was a party in progress with members of the American film colony in London (this was the period of the first Hollywood colonisation of the British industry), and that he found himself in a quarrel with an actor who was impugning the supposed 'toughness' of the East Enders. Chaplin's reflections on the evening were that he 'was right here in the midst of my youth, but somehow I seemed apart from it. I felt as though I was viewing it under a glass. It could be seen all too plainly, but when I reached to touch it it was not there – only the glass could be felt, this glass that had been glazed by the years since I left ...

'A man cannot go back. He thinks he can, but other things have happened to his life. He has new ideas, new friends, new attachments. He doesn't belong to his past, except that the past has, perhaps, made marks on him.'

The present, certainly, was making inordinate claims upon him. In his first three days in London he received 73,000 letters or postcards. Well over one third of these, he reckoned, were begging letters asking for sums from £1 to £1000. Another large group insulted him for his failure to serve in the armed forces during the war, and sent him white feathers. He was distressed by these but somewhat consoled by others from ex-servicemen thanking him for what he had done for their morale with his films. One of them sent him the medals he had won at the front, because, he said, Chaplin's contribution to the war made his own seem so insignificant.

The much publicised visit to London permitted Chaplin to revisit his past; and to the end of his life he was to make sentimental journeys to the places of his boyhood. Yet at the same time it was definitively borne in on him that he was now permanently committed to the world of those whom he (how ironically?) called 'The Immortals'. He described his shyness and awkwardness and sense of being only a dull listener at a dinner party where the guests included Knoblock and Edwin Lutyens, whom Chaplin (discreetly not naming him) evidently found a somewhat loud buffoon whose humour he could not himself follow. The host was E. V. Lucas, who some years before had been one of the first serious writers to discuss Chaplin's films and to point out the quality of pathos and even tragedy that lay so close to the humour in them. The veteran actor Sir Squire Bancroft, who was rumoured never to have seen a film, revealed that in Chaplin's honour he had just been to see *Shoulder Arms*; and said flattering things about the sequence in which Chaplin reads another soldier's letter over his shoulder to share the emotions that this luckier comrade experiences in his news from Blighty. Sir James Barrie said that he would like Chaplin to play Peter Pan; but the comedian was too overcome by shyness and the extent of the compliment to discuss the offer. Later he and Barrie escaped to the latter's apartment where they were joined by the popular actor Gerald du Maurier.

Another evening was spent in mutual admiration with H. G. Wells, with whom he talked about Soviet Russia, and who was struck by his off-screen elegance, and his power of observation. Chaplin countered that 'Whatever keenness of perception I have is momentary, fleeting. I observe all in ten minutes, or not at all.' He spent an evening in Limehouse with Thomas Burke whose melodramatic stories of darkest London were then much in vogue (one of them had inspired D. W. Griffith's *Broken Blossoms*). Burke, said Chaplin 'is the one man who sees London through the same kind of glasses as myself'. Burke was a small, taciturn man; but Chaplin appreciated his guided tour in which he silently pointed out the landmarks with his stick. 'He has given me the stories before. Now he is telling them over in pictures.'

Throughout the book there is a sense that the competing attractions of the nostalgic past and the illustrious present imposed a special strain upon Chaplin; and impulsively he decided to leave London for Paris. The ruse of retaining the apartment at the Ritz and the secretaries who battled there daily with the vast correspondence, failed to cover his steps; and he arrived in France, somewhat seasick, to find the same armies of reporters. It was if anything some relief that he did not speak their language; though whenever he was able to understand them, he found that they were asking the same questions as the reporters everywhere else: he speculated that the American newsmen had simply radioed on a list of the stock questions.

Paris could also be importunate in its memories: 'The Folies Bergères seems shabbier. I remember having played here once myself with a pantomime act. How grand it looked then. Rather antiquated now. Somehow it saddened me, this bit of memory that was chased up before me.' But celebrity eclipsed nostalgia. He was feted by the Sassoons and the Rocksavages; met Lady Astor, Georges Carpentier and Jacques Copeau, and went to a mannequin show. A visit to a bohemian cabaret was to serve him well when it came to creating Parisian colour for *A Woman of Paris*, made a couple of years after the visit.

Chaplin and Carl Robinson next moved on to a Berlin that was still recovering from the shocks of war and revolution, and in the throes of Expressionism in art and inflation in the economy. Chaplin's experiences there exemplified an ancient show-business joke. At first relaxed and relieved to find himself unrecognized, since his films had not yet been released in Germany, he soon found himself becoming uneasy. Only as more and more expatriate Americans saw and acclaimed him, and, most notably, when he was noticed and courted by Pola Negri, the greatest German star of the day, who was very shortly to be lured to Hollywood, was he able, as he said, to secure draught-free tables in Berlin restaurants.

Chaplin returned to London without much regret for Berlin – even if he was much struck by the voluptuous Miss Negri. His social life now built up to an absurd crescendo. He flew to Paris for the première of *The Kid*; and the audience was a cross-section of cosmopolitan elite, with Vanderbilts and Stuyvesants, Cecile Sorel and Georges Carpentier, and representatives of every area of politics, diplomacy, the arts and aristocracy. The guests also included Henri Letellier, a celebrated financier and *bon vivant* who was to provide Chaplin with the original of Pierre Revel in *A Woman of Paris*.

After the show, Chaplin received a decoration from the French Government; then flew back to London to arrive too late for a rendezvous with Lloyd George.

Later social engagements in England had also included country weekends with H. G. Wells and the discreetly flamboyant Sir Philip Sassoon who had a suite redecorated in his home in Chaplin's preferred colours. The visit to Sassoon, however, gave Chaplin further cause for reflection on the privileges, potential and penalties of his fame. When he accompanied Sassoon to the dedication of a war memorial in the local church, he was distressed that excitement over his presence inevitably detracted from the solemnity of the occasion. On a visit to a hospital for the war wounded, he was touched and impressed at his power to bring gaiety to the spirits of these irretrievably wrecked men.

Attempting to the end to keep his slipping hold upon his past, he spent his final night with his cousin Aubrey, and insisted on visiting Aubrey's public house: 'I must get him more custom.' The melancholy of his departure (he promised to return the next year, but it was a decade before he came back to London) was quickly overtaken by the excitements of his return to the United States:

'Going over it all, it has been so worth while and the job ahead of me looks worth while. If I can bring smiles to the tired eyes in Kennington and Whitechapel, if I have absorbed and understood the virtues and problems of those simpler people I have met, and if I have gathered the least bit of inspiration from those greater personages who were kind to me, then this has been a wonderful trip, and somehow I am eager to get back to work and begin paying for it.'

The Gold Rush *1925*.

Opinion of the Twenties

In the teens of the century, the public of the entire world had elevated Charles Chaplin to a status and idolatry no artist in any medium had ever known before. The twenties were to see the consolidation of his reputation among the intellectuals and critics of every nation. In the six years from 1914 and 1919 he had made something in the region of thirty hours of film, bursting with invention and creativity. The seven feature films he was to make in the next decade were to include some of his most accomplished and impeccable work.

All Chaplin's films after 1918 were made in his own studio, which permitted him the freedom and concentration he required. The eighteen month period in which he was supposed, under his contract with First National, to deliver eight pictures, finally extended to five years. When the twenties began he still owed First National four films. The first of these was *The Kid*, a singular combination of uncompromised nineteenth century melodrama and Chaplin's most inspired comedy. In the serious, even tragic story that underlies the comic surfaces it is easy to see Chaplin's very personal memories of late Victorian London. For 1921 there was no little courage in Chaplin's unqualified defence of the unmarried mother, played by Edna Purviance: 'Her only sin – motherhood' says a title. The mother, abandoned by her artist lover, leaves her new-born child in an opulent car, with a note asking the finder to be kind to the foundling. By the time she repents of her decision to leave the child and commit suicide, it is too late, the car has been stolen by thieves, who in turn leave the child in a back alley where it is found by the little tramp, Charlie. When his attempts to pass on his find to someone else fail, he reluctantly adopts it, improvising ingenious nursery equipment such as cradles, diapers, feeding bottles and potties.

Five years later tramp and child are rediscovered living happily in a hovel as father and son, and also business partners: the kid goes around breaking windows, followed by the tramp who thus secures regular trade as a glazier.

The mother, meanwhile, has become rich and famous as an opera singer; and diverts her frustrated maternal instincts to charitable work among the children of the slums. It is thus that, unknowing, she meets her own child; and ironically it is due to her concern over his sickness that the unorthodox

The Kid *1921. Chaplin with Jackie Coogan.*

family relationship is brought to the attention of the authorities who consequently attempt to have the child placed in an orphanage. After comic and
tear-jerking adventures, the child is eventually restored to his mother and
the tramp, presumably, is suitably rewarded. A curious interpolated dream
sequence in which the tramp envisions the slums transformed into a heaven
peopled with angel-metamorphoses of the familiar and feared denizens, was
criticized by no less an authority on whimsy than Sir James Barrie, when
he first met Chaplin in London shortly after the film's release. Chaplin
defended the scene, saying that it had been inspired by Barrie's own play
A Kiss for Cinderella.

Six reels long (ninety minutes screen time at the normal running speed
adopted by projectionists at the period) *The Kid* was the longest film Chaplin
had directed until that date. The production had also been very costly; and
it was only after considerable wrangling that First National were persuaded
to revise the original terms of their agreement so as fairly to reimburse
Chaplin, as producer, for his expenditure. In the end both the company and
Chaplin were to profit handsomely from the film.

Chaplin's co-star was the infant Jackie Coogan, whose extraordinary
appeal and talent was clearly an inspiration for the film. Chaplin had originally seen him on stage, taking part in his father's vaudeville act as an eccentric
dancer. The child – first tested in a small role in *A Day's Pleasure* – proved
phenomenally responsive to Chaplin's skill and patience in schooling him.
Little Coogan's later career, and notably his performance as *Oliver Twist*,
showed however that his talent was no fluke or dependent solely on one
director of genius.

After *The Kid*, Chaplin's next two films, *The Idle Class* and *Pay Day*,
both in two reels, were necessarily an anti-climax, a return to an uncompli-
cated comedy style devoid of the deeper, even tragic resonances of his first
feature-length production. The title of *The Idle Class* is somewhat equivocal,
and could refer to either of Chaplin's two roles, as a young alcoholic millionaire and as a hobo, the rich man's double. When the tramp chances in at
a fancy dress party at the house of the millionaire, there is a predictable
comedy of confusions involving the millionaire's exasperated wife, family
and guests. In *Pay Day* Chaplin's Little Fellow is for once a working man,
with a home and wife. The film shows him at work and having difficulties
with his tough foreman and the foreman's attractive daughter; on payday,
making his way home somewhat the worse for a drink or two and mistaking
a hot dog wagon for a streetcar; and finally returning home to his shrewish
wife and a chilly night's sleep in the bath.

Chaplin's last film for First National distribution was a brilliant return
to form. *The Pilgrim* was in four reels, and so ran for rather more than
an hour at silent projection speeds. Charlie is an escaped convict, who changes
his prison stripes for the clothes of a bather. These turn out to be the attire
of a clergyman, and Charlie is mistaken for the new parson due to arrive
at a tiny rural community. Chaplin's satirical reflections on religious bigotry,

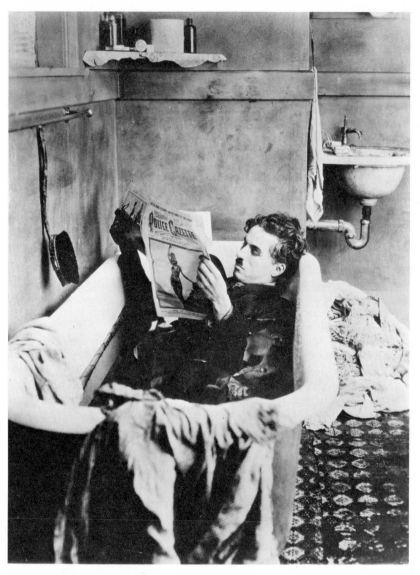

Pay Day *1922: one of the rare films which shows Chaplin in (relative) domesticity.*

puritanism and comparative morality (he, the escaped criminal disguised as a preacher, worsts the villains who have robbed the young heroine) are shrewd; and the film has some of his most memorable scenes – his mimed sermon on David and Goliath; his confrontation with a terrible child; and the concluding scene of the film, making his usual waddling exit towards the horizon, but this time straddling the border between the United States, where he is wanted by the law, and Mexico, where the peace is threatened by pistol-popping bandits.

The Pilgrim concluded his contract with First National Distributors; and Chaplin was finally free to make a film for release by United Artists, the distribution company he had formed in 1919 with D. W. Griffith, Douglas Fairbanks and Mary Pickford, to ensure the most advantageous release of their own productions.

Chaplin took the momentous and courageous decision to make a serious dramatic picture, in which he would not appear. Partly this decision seems to have originated in his promise to launch Edna Purviance, his loyal leading lady through seven years and more than thirty films, as a dramatic actress. He had cast around for some suitably stately roles for Edna, who, though still beautiful, was fast growing matronly in form. He considered *The Trojan Women*, then a film about the Empress Josephine. Then in the summer of 1922 a meeting with the original 'gold digger', Peggy Hopkins Joyce, suggested the idea of *A Woman of Paris*.

Edna plays Marie St Clair, who lives with her tyrannical father in a little French village. Her boyfriend Jean helps her escape from the house for an evening walk; but on their return the father will not let the girl in. Nor will Jean's father permit her to remain in his house.

Marie and Jean decide to elope to Paris; but Jean fails to meet Marie at the station, because his father has suddenly died from a heart attack. So Marie sets off to Paris alone, to become, only a year later, the glittering but discontented mistress of Pierre Revel, a rich playboy. By chance she meets Jean again: he has come to Paris with his mother, to work as a struggling artist. Marie commissions him to paint her portrait. They fall in love again; and Jean proposes marriage. Marie decides to leave Pierre; but then overhears the weak-willed Jean telling his possessive mother that he is not serious in saying he will marry her. Marie returns to Pierre and refuses to see the now remorseful and distraught Jean. In despair, Jean shoots himself. His mother sets out with his gun to avenge herself on Marie; but is softened and reconciled when she finds the girl weeping over the body of Jean.

The film had triumphant premières in Hollywood and New York, and a critical reception more unanimously enthusiastic than has been accorded to practically any other film before or since. To Chaplin's horror, however, the film proved a failure at the box-office. Clearly the public wanted their idol to give them comedies; and they wanted to see him in them. So great was Chaplin's disappointment when this masterly work was spurned, that he quickly withdrew it from circulation, and only relented, to add a musical

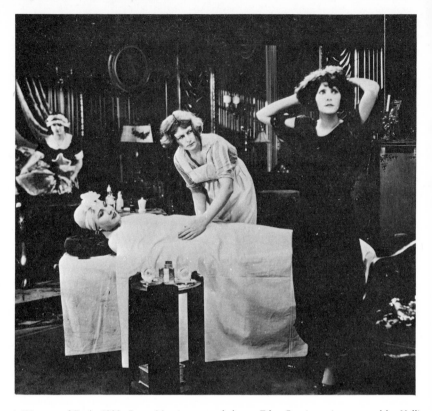

A Woman of Paris *1923. Betty Morrissey stands by as Edna Purviance is massaged by Nellie Bly Baker, who was not a professional actress but Chaplin's secretary.*

sound track and re-edit it for reissue, at the very end of his life, in 1976.

Twenty-two months after the première of *A Woman of Paris*, however, Chaplin released what was to be his most popular and profitable picture, *The Gold Rush*. He claimed that the idea for the film had come to him one day when he was visiting Douglas Fairbanks and Mary Pickford, and saw a stereoscope slide of gold prospectors in the Chilcoot Pass. Further inspiration came from the macabre story of the Donner Party disaster of 1846, when pioneers snowbound in the Sierra Nevada were forced to feed on the corpses of their dead companions.

Chaplin seems to have created his elaborate and costly sets – he covered plaster mountains with hundreds of tons of false snow – and then allowed the scenario and comic business to grow out of them. For the opening shot, a spectacular image of an endless line of prospectors, stretching as far as the eye can see and picked out against the white, snow-covered mountain side, Chaplin took his crew to Truckee, California, and transported a train-

A Woman of Paris *1923: a novel striptease in Bohemian Paris.*

load of five hundred hobo extras from Sacramento.

The role of the dance-hall girl with whom Chaplin's Little Fellow falls in love, was originally intended for Lita Gray who, as a twelve-year-old had appeared in *The Kid* and had acted a small role, alongside her mother, in *The Idle Class*. Before the film was begun, however, Miss Gray had become Mrs Chaplin; and the role went to the charming Georgia Hale, whose most significant previous performance had been in Josef von Sternberg's first film, *The Salvation Hunters.*

In *The Gold Rush* Chaplin's tramp has become a lone prospector who is literally blown by the blizzards of the frozen north into the company of Black Larsen, a villain of darkest hue, and Big Jim McKay, who has struck gold. Lots are drawn and Larsen goes off to seek food. The others, beleaguered in the hut by snow, are threatened with starvation. Big Jim has alarming hallucinations that Charlie is a plump and juicy chicken; later the two solemnly boil Charlie's boot. In the justly famous sequence that follows, Chaplin devours the sole of the boot as if it were the choicest delicacy, deftly picking out the nails with the expertise of a connoisseur.

Eventually the storm abates and they go their separate ways. Big Jim meets Larsen, who has discovered and taken possession of Jim's gold strike. In the fight for possession, Big Jim is struck over the head and loses his memory; and Larsen goes on to his death in an avalanche. Meanwhile Charlie arrives

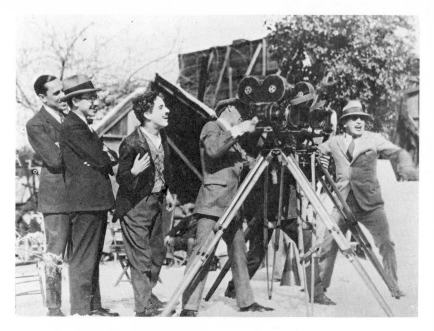

Chaplin directs The Gold Rush. *The admiring bystanders have not been identified, but their light clothing shows that the filming was taking place in the studio and not on location.*

at a little mining town, where he sees and falls in love with Georgia, the dance hall girl, who pretends to encourage his advances merely in order to affront a too confident suitor. In another celebrated sequence, Chaplin (now caretaking the hut of a kindly prospector) prepares a Thanksgiving dinner for Georgia and her friends. When they forget to come, he drops asleep at the table and dreams of the dinner he had hoped for, providing a climax to the entertainment with the brilliant dance routine he performs with two bread rolls, representing big boots, stuck on the end of forks.

The amnesiac Big Jim arrives in town, recognizes Charlie and promises him half his riches if only he can remember where his gold mine lies. Their return to the wilderness provides the opportunity for a further series of comic variations in the hut, which is blown by the blizzard to the edge of a precipice where, delicately poised, it responds to every movement of the men inside, finally plunging thousands of feet at the very moment that Charlie, the last out, jumps to safety.

A final scene shows the two men, now millionaires, on board a ship bound for home. For the benefit of press photographers, Charlie takes off his fur coat, and dresses up in the tramp costume of his poverty-stricken past. Thus attired he chances to fall down a trap into the steerage section of the vessel, where he is discovered by Georgia. When the shabby figure is mistaken for

The Gold Rush *1925*.

The Circus *1928*.

a stowaway, Georgia offers to pay his passage. The misunderstandings are cleared up, and the press men ask Charlie who Georgia is. He delightedly whispers to them that she is his fiancée.

At the conclusion of *The Gold Rush* Chaplin's professional and private reputation were at zenith. Just over a year later, however, came his divorce from Lita Gray. Lita's lawyer uncle drew up a list of complaints on her behalf which delighted scandal mongers of the twenties. When the financial settlement was delayed, a great deal of publicity was given to Chaplin's alleged failure to provide for his two baby sons; and women's organizations insultingly set up a fund to assist the mother and children. Chaplin was pilloried almost as viciously as he would be two decades later over the Joan Barry affair. H. L. Mencken – himself no particular admirer of Chaplin – reflected, 'The very morons who worshipped Charlie Chaplin six weeks ago now prepare to dance around the stake while he is burned.'

It was in such unhappy and anxious circumstances that Chaplin embarked on and completed *The Circus*, eventually released in January 1928. His leading lady, Merna Kennedy, was a friend of Lita Gray; the juvenile lead Harry

The Circus *1928. Chaplin with Henry Bergman.*

Crocker, who was also Chaplin's assistant, was a former Hearst newspaper-man. The film enjoyed a favourable reception, despite the surrounding personal circumstances; and indeed Chaplin won a special 'Oscar' (his only Academy Award until the special honour accorded to him in 1972) for his 'versatility and genius in writing, acting, directing and producing *The Circus*'. Although this film has generally been overshadowed by the two that preceded and followed it, *The Gold Rush* and *City Lights*, it is, seen today, a brisk, enjoyable and exceptionally well composed comedy.

It was generally referred to as Chaplin's 'Pagliacci story'. A complete circus and menagerie were hired and kept on the payroll for a year. As with *The Gold Rush* Chaplin seems to have drawn inspiration from the setting. The tramp is first seen in the carnival attached to the circus, in a series of adventures with a pickpocket and his victims, a fun house and a hall of mirrors. Finally, attempting to evade his pursuers, Charlie rushes into the circus ring during the performance of an illusionist and delights the audience by ruining all the man's tricks. Since the circus is rapidly going broke, a new comic attraction is welcomed; but Charlie proves to be comic only when he does not intend to be so. However, by concealing from him that he is the comedy star of the show, the circus proprietor succeeds in building him into a box office hit.

Meanwhile Charlie falls in love with the ill-treated daughter of the bullying circus proprietor, a bareback rider. The romance prospers, despite incidents with a lion and other hazards of the circus, until the arrival of a new and handsome aerial artiste. Charlie sadly but resignedly yields up his romance; and is left alone on the scarred ring of grass left behind by the circus as it moves on.

*   *   *

Since Harvey O'Higgins's pioneer study of Chaplin as an artist, the most august critics, who might otherwise never even see films, let alone write about them, were prepared to write seriously about Chaplin's art – and this term too had in the twenties only recently been applied to the movies. Not until the thirties was a book published in English devoted to critical study of Chaplin (if the English translation of Delluc's *Charlot* is excluded); but in other countries the trickle of Chaplin books had begun. In France Delluc's study was followed by a volume, *Charlot*, in the series Disque Vert (1924), Edouard Raymond's *La Passion de Charlie Chaplin* (1927), Henri Poullaille's *Charles Chaplin* and Robert Florey's *Charlie Chaplin*. In Germany there were Gerhard Ausleger's *Charlie Chaplin* (1924) and Erich Burger's *Charlie Chaplin: Bericht Seines Lebens*. In the Soviet Union the distinguished writer and critic Viktor Shklovski published a monograph, *Chaplin* (1923).

Of this group, Robert Florey's book is perhaps the most representative and the most interesting because of Florey's long-sustained enthusiasm for Chaplin and his later association with him. French-born, Florey arrived in

Hollywood in 1921, when he was twenty-one, and worked as a journalist, sending back articles on Hollywood and its personalities to the French press. Later he became a director in his own right, his most important films including *The Cocoanuts* (1929), *The Murders in the Rue Morgue* (1932) and *The Beast With Five Fingers* (1946).Later in life he directed hundreds of television films. His idolatry for Chaplin survived the years; and he leapt at the chance to be an associate director on *Monsieur Verdoux* – an experience of which he left an account in his *Hollywood d'hier et d'aujourd'hui*.

His *Charlie Chaplin* was written at the end of 1926 and in the first days of 1927, and appeared in a series *Les Grands Artistes de l'Ecran* (other volumes of which were dedicated to Valentino, Pola Negri, Ivan Mosjoukine and Adolphe Menjou). His principal informant about the early years of Chaplin's career was Chaplin's business manager, Alf Reeves. A mere twelve years after Chaplin's entry into films, however, memories had already faded, and Florey's dates are culpably inaccurate. The book is more valuable for its first-hand impressions of Chaplin at work; and Florey gives a cutting sequence for the lion scene of *The Circus* which at the time was still in production. He is also able to pass on anecdotes of Chaplin's collaborators; and such sidelights as that Chaplin's regularly revived project for a film on Napoleon had just been set aside once again, because of the news of Abel Gance's epic production.

An appreciative preface by Lucien Wahl begins: 'Charlot is a miracle. He is perhaps a unique instance, certainly exceptional. All who see him approve and admire. Everywhere he is recognized as a great artist, much more, a creator, in every country and in every class of society. That is the miracle.'

Wahl goes on to elucidate this reflection: 'The miracle of Charlot is to have brought into communion people who think quite differently. He makes it possible for masses of people to believe that they understand one another, even though they are perfect strangers one to another.' Wahl also postulates various persons' explanations of the special attractions of Chaplin. Among the most interesting he quotes are, 'I prefer not to analyse anything. I experience the charm of a new force. I sense a genius comparable to Shakespeare even though I cannot compare the two. The great farce with the moving sadness produce in me a mixture of sorrow and joy. That is the power of Charlot; his originality is what he achieves through silence on the screen. With Charlot the musical accompaniment fades, and I no longer even notice the decor ...' Again, 'He never makes me laugh, but his superb eyes make me live with him as long as he is on the screen.'

In the United States, one of the earliest and most sensitive efforts to assess Chaplin's achievement in elevating slapstick to serious uses is, unfortunately, unsigned. It appeared in the publication *Exceptional Photoplays*, which was published by the National Board of Review and prepared by a committee. Some of the reviews were signed; but the January/February 1921 review of *The Kid* was not. Internal evidence suggests that it may at least in part be attributed to Alfred B. Kuttner, chairman of the National Board of Review, who wrote on film for *The Nation* and *The New Republic* (and so may have wished to avoid signing articles on the same film in too many publications) and was also – cf. the reference to Goethe – a translator from German literature:

'The most outstanding figure in our moving picture world is an Englishman who seems to have found this country entirely congenial and who has never used his leisure moments to dash off a book to tell the world what he thinks of America. Instead he has put much sweat and labor into giving us a criticism of life. To do this he has relied upon a trick mustache, a small bamboo cane, a tilted derby, a pair of enormously large, flat shoes, and a pair of the most ominously threatening yet never quite descending pair of trousers in which mortal man has ever dared to walk forth. These have been, so to speak, his artistic resources, and with them he can bring tears of laughter to the largest audience in the world with less apparent effort than any other actor on the screen.

'Charles Chaplin's method is what is commonly called "slapstick". The term is used in disparagement. In many quarters Chaplin is considered very lowbrow, very vulgar, very unaesthetic. The endless beatings which he gives and takes, his tumbles and recoveries, his waddling walk, are not accepted in the upper circles. That is, they are not officially accepted, for it is very curious how surreptitious many people are about what they really enjoy in a picture. They will often roar their heads off and then turn up their noses. They say it is nothing but "slapstick", and that seems to anger them enormously.

'You would think that slapstick had been invented in the movies. It happens, however, that slapstick has been used to entertain mankind ever since monkeys started to throw cocoanuts at each other. The classics are full of it. The *Don Quixote* of Cervantes contains more slapstick than all the movie comedies thus far made. The comedies of Aristophanes are so full of the frankest kind of slapstick that only scholars of the chastest reputation are allowed to read them in the original. Suppose you were to put Falstaff and the Merry Wives of Windsor into a movie, would you cut out the slapstick? Goethe would laugh at you. Think of the tricks he made Doctor Faust play. Yet these antics are often cause for disapproval in the movies.

'The plain fact of the matter is that it is quite absurd to criticize an artistic method if the effect is genuine. Laughter is achieved by incongruities and distortions. On the screen this must be done in terms of action. If you can upset the bumptious hero by making him slip on a banana peel or ruffle a false sublimity by tickling it with a feather, you are producing valid satire. Pity often lurks in the ludicrous just as much as in the pathetic. Watch Chaplin closely and you find that, when he wishes, he can be a master of irony.

'Something of this revolt against the dishonor of slapstick must have been in his mind when he made *The Kid*. He is telling the story of a foundling who is taken in by an itinerant mender of window panes and is reared to young boyhood. He does not alter his method, though he refines it. There

The Gold Rush *1925*.

is still lots of rough-and-tumble. But there is also more feeling, and more understanding of childhood, than in a hundred *Little Lord Fauntleroys*. Slapstick triumphs over sentimentality.'

The more sophisticated the critics, the better pleased they seemed to be with *The Kid*. In *The New Republic*, one of the magazine's founder-editors Francis Hackett, the Irish-born critic and historian, concluded that the wisdom, sincerity and integrity which Chaplin exhibited in the film should have gone 'some way to revolutionize motion picture production in this country. From an industry *The Kid* raises production to an art. An art it should be, in spite of the long-suffering public.'

Hackett most of all admired *The Kid* for form, a quality which, like Sunday newspapers, Golden Oak furniture, Yonkers carpets and 'the snub-nosed and stub-toed Ford car', American films notably lacked. Form and integrity transcended the essential, old-fashioned thinness of the anecdote, with its dependence on melodrama coincidence. Equally Chaplin's exactitude of taste ensured that sentimentality was always corrected by comedy, whilst the very violations of good taste were turned to grotesque account. It is interesting that Hackett especially admires the dream sequence which Sir James Barrie so firmly disapproved. Its quality, he suggests, is the very limitedness and meagreness of the vision. 'It was like a simple man's version of the Big Change, made up from the few properties with which a simple man would be likely to be acquainted.' This ability of Chaplin's to embody the visions of a limited imagination, 'the simplified Heaven of the antic sprite whom Chaplin has created', relates to a paradox in Chaplin's creativity which Hackett seems to have been the first to point out: the ability to represent the supremely *ordinary* human, 'all the more marvellous when one remembers that Chaplin is not a projection of the average, but a variation, a sport'.

It has already been noted that *A Woman of Paris* attracted a critical enthusiasm such as few films have enjoyed. Throughout the world's press there seems to have been no dissenting voice. Chaplin was freely compared to Hardy, to de Maupassant, to Ibsen – though generally they thought him a good deal better than Ibsen, because having long demonstrated that comedy is never far removed from tragedy, he now showed that tragedy could have its share of gaiety. Robert Sherwood, who considered that 'there is more real genius in Charles Chaplin's *A Woman of Paris* than in any picture I have ever seen' said that he had 'caught and conveyed the contrast between joy and sorrow which makes existence in this terrestrial ball as interesting as it is'. When the film arrived in Britain in early 1924, *The Manchester Guardian* called it 'the greatest modern story that the screen has yet seen ... He has had the courage to throw the sum total of screen conventions on the scrap heap.' Again the perceptive writer in *Exceptional Photoplays* remained anonymous: *A Woman of Paris*, he (or she) wrote, 'is one of the few, in the strictly artistic sense, fine motion pictures which have been produced since that potential art developed into an industry.

'In *A Woman of Paris* Mr Chaplin as a writer and director has not done

A Woman of Paris *1923. Marie (Edna Purviance, right), now a courtesan, meets her former lover, the artist Jean (Carl Miller) and his mother (Lydia Knott).*

anything radical or anything esoteric; he has merely used his intelligence to the highest degree, an act which has ceased to be expected of motion picture people for many years. He has written and directed a story in which all the characters act upon motives which the spectator immediately recognizes as natural and sincere, and therefore *A Woman of Paris* breathes an atmosphere of reality, and thereby holds the attention of any perceptive audience in thrall.

'As a director Mr Chaplin has attained to a great achievement, because he has succeeded in contributing his own fascinating personality and subtle intelligence to his actors in their given situation. The performance of Edna Purviance as the woman of Paris is a thing of much charm, altogether aside from her physical loveliness. The outstanding feature of the picture is the charm and natural goodness she makes convincing in spite of her relations to Pierre Revel, as played by Adolphe Menjou with great distinction. This relation of Marie and Pierre Revel is undeniably in conflict with the thesis that a union outside of marriage is invariably unhappy, is always entirely a thing of the flesh, and involves indecency of mind. Marie and Pierre, while estranged in the end, are never violently sorrowful and they are certainly not excessively fleshy. Also, their feelings, if these are an indication of their state of mind, are ones of genuine affection and respect for each other. It would be wiser to say about this attachment that it is a plea for charity and understanding of such people by one who is charitable and understands them, than that it is a subtle stroke at the wholesomeness and desirability of marriage and lawful love. For the emotional disaster that overtakes Marie is due to her desire for lawful love and marriage, and in Pierre there is always an implied sympathy for the want in Marie's heart, as well as an urge to satisfy it. That this should be part of the drama of so fine a technical achievement will doubtless be regrettable to many, and a point for attack on the picture as a whole. On the other hand, there will be many who will perceive a treatment both clean and honest, a purpose both artistic and truthful. Not a spot in this polished picture is tarnished by anything cheap and vulgar, not one moment is spent in pandering to low tastes or the craving for the sensational.'

'*A Woman of Paris* has the one quality almost every other motion picture that has been made to date lacks – restraint. The acting is moving without ever being fierce; the story is simple and realistic without ever being inane; the settings are pleasing and adequate without ever being colossally stupid. The result is a picture of dignity and intelligence, and the effect is startling because it is so unusual.

'The achievement of Mr Chaplin indicates what should be obvious, that 10,000 in the cast do not necessarily make a moving drama, and directors of pictures made on that principle would do well to see this picture often and take it to heart if it is the artistic motion picture that they are striving for. The action is very simple, and to tell the story would be unprofitable, because the story is not at all unusual, which is the very thing that makes it humanly interesting. But to attain the simplicity and even flow which his picture has must have cost Mr Chaplin much effort ...'

By the time of *The Gold Rush* (the film by which, said Chaplin, he would most wish to be remembered), even the most eminent literary figures did not disdain critical discussion of his pictures. In Britain, Arnold Bennett set down some forthright views on Hollywood in an article on *The Film 'Story'* contributed to the December 1927 issue of *Close Up*:

'As regards the artistic future of the film, it would not matter – provided that Chaplin were saved – if all Hollywood were swallowed up in an earthquake. The loss of life would be terrible and deplorable; the domestic tragedies would be agonizing; tens of millions of simple souls would sincerely mourn in five continents, but the artistic future of the film would not suffer in the

A Woman of Paris *1923. Edna Purviance swoons in the arms of Adolphe Menjou.*

slightest degree. I have never – Chaplin's work apart – seen a good American film. I have rarely seen one that was not artistically revolting. Not one of the famous American directors has left a permanent mark on film history, or produced anything that would not deeply grieve the judicious.

'I must specially except Charles Chaplin, who, in addition to being a great actor, is a great producer. *The Gold Rush*, while not perfect in some essential matters, was a great film. It would bear seeing twice.'

In the United States, Edmund Wilson, already revered as a man of letters, wrote the review in *The New Republic*. Wilson's approach is predictably analytical. Examining 'gag' construction as the basis of American silent film comedy, he goes on to show that Chaplin is the superior of his contemporaries, first because he is his own gag writer, so that his 'gags' have always 'an unmistakable quality of personal fancy'; and second, by reference to the gag sequence of the hut perched precariously on the edge of a cliff in *The Gold Rush*, he demonstrates Chaplin's unmatched ability to develop his comedy with steady logic and vivid imagination'.

At the same time, however, Wilson feels that despite Chaplin's sophistication in combining his gags with the ironic, the pathetic or the romantic situation, he has failed to keep step with his rivals in the development of slapstick comedy. He continues, he says, with the old, cheap trappings and simple tricks. Chaplin is more old fashioned even than the most old-fashioned movies: he is as old-fashioned as Karno's music hall sketch company in which he learned his business. 'As the comedy of the movies has come more and more to depend on machinery and stunts, Charlie Chaplin has remained incorrigibly a pantomimist' (which one might have thought no bad thing).

Wilson's consequent speculations on Chaplin's artistic future are especially interesting, since they embody much of the criticism that was to be levelled more often ten or twenty years later, after *Modern Times* and *Monsieur Verdoux*. Only a couple of years earlier critics had hailed the artistic revolution of *A Woman of Paris*; Wilson however predicts that he is unlikely to play an important role in the artistic developments of the future. Chaplin's gift is primarily the actor's, not the artist's or the director's: 'All the photographic and plastic side of the movies, which is at present making such remarkable advances, seems not to interest Chaplin.' His pictures, he says, are as raw almost as *Tillie's Punctured Romance*.

Edmund Wilson conceded, nevertheless, that 'In the meantime, it may be that his present series of pictures – *The Kid*, *The Pilgrim* and *The Gold Rush* – with their gags and their overtones of tragedy, their adventures half absurd, half realistic, their mythical hero, now a figure of poetry, now a type out of the funny papers, represent the height of his achievement. He could scarcely do better in any field than in the best moments of these creations.'

While some critics of the time missed the poetry and pathos of *The Gold Rush* in *The Circus*, others seem to have been positively relieved at this lack. Alexander Bakshy, who reviewed *The Circus* for *The Nation*, was a distinguished Russo-English critic who had been writing on films since 1913. He found Chaplin 'again at his very best', even though the rest of the actors were no more than competent and the direction of the picture in general was without distinction. Bakshy congratulated himself that Chaplin had proved the truth of a prediction he had made in an article written fifteen years before, in which he said that the legitimate actors should leave the cinematograph screen to the dancers, clowns and acrobats, 'who do know something about the laws of movement'.

Chaplin, he said, was the perfect clown and acrobat, and 'by way of confirming my dictum at once leapt to such heights of artistic distinction that

The Circus *1928. Charlie shares his sandwich with the hungry equestrienne (Merna Kennedy).*

ever since there have been only two kinds of motion picture actors: Charlie Chaplin and the rest'. The classification, he said, was based not merely on the singularity of Chaplin's genius, but equally on the singularity of his methods as an actor. 'Chaplin's mannerisms, the peculiar traits of the screen character he has created, have been imitated and plagiarised times without number. On the other hand, his consistent pantomime acting (I cannot recall a single picture in which Chaplin moves his lips as if actually speaking), his emphasis on expressive movement (his gait, for instance) and his puppet-like, essentially non-realistic treatment of his role – these are the characteristics of Chaplin's acting which have found but few imitators, and certainly none to show anything like Chaplin's appreciation of their meaning and importance.

In *The New Republic The Circus* was reviewed by Stark Young, normally the journal's dramatic critic. Young admired the film even while criticizing Chaplin for the too calculated effect of pathos in the final scene. 'Such effects as this will carry Charlie Chaplin's pathos to a wider public, no doubt, and so may serve to add to him a slightly different sort of popularity. But the whole world, often unconsciously perhaps, has already felt his pathos in its truest kind, and the scene mars what has just gone before ... he has no need of that sort of fact'.

More interesting however is the attempt of Young, who evidently knew Chaplin personally, to present an intellectual portrait of the man and artist, endeavouring to reconcile some of the apparent contradictions. He began his essay by quoting the opinion of a friend of Byron's that a good part of his fascination arose from the power he had of 'a certain dangerous intimacy'.

'I have often thought of that observation with regard to Charlie Chaplin. When you talk with him you sense at the very start an impulse to make the connection between the two of you direct and alive, a hunger that the moment should be pure and glowing, and the exchange between you and him open like a passage in art.

'As we talk, I always have a sense that there is much that is not coming into what is said, facts, if you like, that are overcrowded, and facts that are so stressed and illuminated as to become different from what they might be for anyone else who knows them. But I never think of this as false, or that the truth is being distorted. I am convinced that it is a high and passionate sincerity that fills this conversation of Charlie Chaplin's, sincerity such as only an imagination like his could come at. I mean that, where exchange and *rapport* between two people, even those who trust each other, is often halting and half-divined, however true it intends to be, this moment between Charlie Chaplin and me, so evolved from his imagination and so driven with the necessity to express himself, has in it a great completeness and absorption; the thing between the two people involved is alive for both, and therefore full of its own truth. He will speak of his personal affairs, of events and of persons that delight, embitter, or destroy him, with a warmth, sting, despondency, exact poetry, or gay wit that is meant to make me see them in the liveliest degree possible, and that, therefore, seeks to engage me through the regions where my response would be most likely and natural. He does not take his colour from me, but from my colour he takes what he needs to express himself to me. He says what he wants me to believe of what he is telling me and, at the same time, I can see that it is what he himself wants to believe of it through me.

'To that talk he gives himself with a fluency and precision and richmindedness that must be rarely equated. The soul of it is shy, but the blood excited; the points are quick and telling; the word sense is remarkable; the variety ranges from a beautiful, warm elevation and eager enthusiasm to the devil's own Rabelaisian articulation, and one of its secrets is that it cannot do without you.

'This complete and shining persuasion and perfect conviction of sympathy and contact could not happen without a sharp air of frankness, or saying anything called for. It needs the sense of a sort of universal lyric candor by which whatever is said seems to be free of the speaker, no longer personal, as moving and alive to the one who hears as to the one who speaks. In Byron this dangerous frankness came from pride, passion, and a vehement sense of his inability to present to the world a just picture of himself, to do "himself justice", as Lady Blessington said. In Charlie Chaplin, shot about by a restless, intense, and fertile mentality, quivering, sensitive, hurt in his early years, proud, egotistical, loving what is gentle, warm, and laureate in life, imprisoned in a mask, this power of frank intimacy was made possible only by an immense success in the world, as life itself was made possible to him by success.'

Fellow Artists

Chaplin rarely, if ever, uttered opinions on fellow comedians. Perhaps he felt that to do so was in some way a breach of professional etiquette. For their part his contemporaries were inclined to speak of him with the awe due to the master of their craft. An exception was the idiosyncratic W. C. Fields; but perhaps there was some oblique compliment even in his snarl: 'The sonofabitch is a goddam ballet dancer.' It is said that Chaplin invited Fields to the première of *Modern Times* and at the end of the show politely saw Fields to his car, only to be rewarded with a valedictory string of obscene abuse. This, too, was in its way a tribute to a talent that could rouse Fields' articulate professional jealousy.

Stan Laurel, quoted in John McCabe's *Charlie Chaplin*, said 'The difference between Charlie and all the rest of us who made comedy – with only one exception, Buster Keaton – was that he just absolutely refused to do anything but the best. To get the best he worked harder than anyone I know.' Keaton, for his part, always spoke of Chaplin's professionalism; and revealed a higher personal regard when he spoke out for Chaplin at the time of Chaplin's political and personal harassment in the early fifties. In the twenty-five years he had known him, he said, he had never heard Chaplin utter a political opinion.

Harold Lloyd, who of all the great silent comedians came nearest to rivalling Chaplin's eminence, told his biographer, William Cahn, 'Charlie was one of the world's great pantomime comedians. He had a tremendous background of training in the English music halls and an innate knowledge of comedy. This gave him a natural bent for timing and spacing ...

'Charlie Chaplin had this sensitivity to an extreme. Like all great comedians, he had an instinct for what was right and just how far he could go. He worked on the borderline between comedy and tragedy. Some of his themes could easily have been dramas, but he pushed them over to the side of comedy.'

One comedian however was nearer than the rest to Chaplin in stature and style. Chaplin is said to have referred to Max Linder as 'his master'; and to have given him a photograph inscribed 'To Max, the Professor, from his disciple, Charles Chaplin.' In those fast-moving infant years of the cinema, the five years' precedence of Linder's career over Chaplin's was more than a whole generation. Linder's origins were very unlike Chaplin's. He was born Gabriel Levielle, in 1882, to a well-to-do family of Saint-Loubes, near Bordeaux. His first ambitions were to be a legitimate stage actor. When he was rejected by the Paris Conservatoire, he joined the company of the Ambigu; and only began to work in films, in 1905, to eke out his salary with a little daytime work. The name Max Linder was adopted to mitigate the shame, for a stage actor, of acting on the screen.

For more than two years, Linder played extra parts in comedy. His chance came when Pathé's major comic star, André Deed, defected to the Italian studios; and Pathé decided to star Max in his own series. Soon Linder had developed and crystallized his screen character of an elegant young boulevardier whose eye for the ladies was always getting him into scrapes. Max broke with the prevailing fashion for comedians, of grotesque and extravagant costumes and make-up, perceiving the rich comedy inherent in the contrast between his personal elegance and sophistication and the absurdity of the situations that befel him. Just like Chaplin, he fought against the frenetic and exaggerated activity of his comic contemporaries, preferring a more developed and carefully observed variety of visual comedy.

Between his debut and 1914 Linder made over four hundred films for Pathé. Inevitably they were uneven – some were crude and repetitious – but they achieved a spectacular international success. In the course of a series of European tours Linder was idolized as only Chaplin, in later years, was to be.

Despite his popularity and huge earnings, however, his life was shadowed. His health, already delicate, was impaired by war service; and his nervous system began to suffer. When Chaplin went to the Mutual Company, Linder was engaged to replace him at the Essanay Company. Although publicly set up as rivals by the competing firms, Chaplin and Linder became friends in private life.

Linder's career at Essanay was short and unsuccessful, and he returned to France. Apparently with Chaplin's encouragement, however, he returned to the United States in 1921 to set up his own company. The three feature films he made – *Seven Years' Bad Luck*, *Be My Wife* and The *Three Must-Get-Theres* – were comic masterpieces, as good as anything in Linder's career, certainly the equal of any comedies then being made in the United States. They were, nevertheless coolly received; and Linder again returned disillusioned to France. After two hesitant attempts to work in feature films, Linder and his young wife died, apparently in a suicide pact, early in the morning of 31st October 1925.

In 1919, between his two visits to the United States, Linder contributed an article to the magazine *Le Film* which, as a rare and singular tribute from one master comedian to another, merits translation in full.

'When you see a film by Charlie Chaplin,' wrote Linder, 'it is easy to

Chaplin with Max Linder, in Hollywood, about 1921.

recognize the amount of work it represents. Even so, however well informed one is, it would be impossible to conceive the continuous and highly intelligent effort of Charlie Chaplin.

'Chaplin has wanted to assure me that it was seeing my films that inspired him to work in the cinema. He calls me his teacher, but I have been the happy one, to take lessons in his school. A lot of nonsense has been talked about Chaplin. First of all, he is English in origin and not French or Spanish as has been said. It was I who first told him that in France he was called Charlot and his brother Sydney, Julot. They were vastly amused by this, and spent the day calling each other these names, with great bursts of laughter. Charlie has been a performer since he was a child. He is a remarkable musician and composer.

'Chaplin has built his own studio in Los Angeles, where he makes his films himself, with the collaboration of his brother and a dozen assistants for the production. Charlie directs with the most minute care. His studio, of course, is equipped with all the most modern improvements, conveniences and apparatus. But the secret does not lie in the mechanical work. It is in the method. Charlie, as a true humourist, has studied laughter, and has achieved a rare precision in evoking it. He leaves nothing to the chance of improvization. He rehearses every scene until he is absolutely satisfied with it. He films every rehearsal and projects them several times, in order to pick out any fault or imperfection that could prejudice the effect he is seeking. He starts over again until he is satisfied, and he is himself harder to please than the most harshly critical of his spectators.

'Until seeing Charlie at work, I never fully realized how unimportant is the amount of film used and the number of times a scene is shot. In France, we count the number of metres shot as if there were some set relation to the length of the finished film. In reality there is a relation only to the quality of the film and the care taken by the director. I will cite some figures to give a precise idea of the quantity of film used. To make a film of 1,800 feet, Chaplin spent two months. He used more than 36,000 feet of negative; that is to say that every scene was shot twenty times. That represents, with trials, alterations, retakes, some fifty rehearsals.

'It has no doubt been noted that Charlie never speaks, and that his films have very few sub-titles. I need not enlarge on his qualities as an actor, for it is sufficient to see one of his films to admire and love them. What is less appreciated is the happy inspiration of his own *mise-en-scène*; a thoughtful and richly gifted director, he knows how to construct and work up his film to bring out his qualities and to emphasize them through all the external action. His gift of observation has already been noted: it is not enough for an actor to express varied sentiments; beyond this it is necessary that the *mise-en-scène* is capable of bringing out and exploiting the gifts of the interpreter. Now Charlie Chaplin knows perfectly how to use himself and his fellow actors to achieve the required note.

'The desired expression comes at the exact moment when it makes its effect. From beginning to end, spectators of every race, of every intelligence, follow the development of his thought down to the most delicate touches of his wit. In *One A.M.* has he not won his wager to keep the audience laughing at the screen during a whole half hour? For that it is very necessary that one is able effortlessly to follow him in the theme he has chosen. Without wishing in any way to diminish his valuable collaborators, it may be truly said that the principal merit of his success is due to him himself, as actor and director. From the day when he became his own director, his films have been on a higher plane of achievement.

'Chaplin works with an obstinate perseverance that is unequalled. Not yet past his early thirties, this man has already silver hairs at his temples.

'In spite of his millions and his fame, he has remained very simple, very friendly and a very good companion. He is on very good terms with the other cinema stars, and is particularly friendly with Douglas Fairbanks, who is himself a charming fellow, and with Mary Pickford, a delightful companion. Chaplin is very gay, I would say almost boyish. His mind always active, and his heart on his sleeve, he is extremely charitable and always ready to contribute to any good works which he is asked to support.

'He never lets anyone come on the set when he is directing. Jealous of his achievement, he is exasperated and annoyed at the same time when, instead of trying to create something new, the other comedians, mostly American, merely try to imitate him, and use cheap tricks to try to get at the secrets of his work. He generously allowed me to watch him work. I can affirm that he has no secrets. He is methodical to an unheard of degree, and he has gifts that defy imitation. He has no tricks, no private inventions, but he is highly intelligent, highly methodical, highly conscientious. It is easy to understand why he wants to keep himself undisturbed when he is shooting, and to avoid his tiresome imitators. He was very unhappy to learn that certain plagiarists in Paris were making use of his name, and he planned to prosecute them. I advised him not to pay them such a tribute. He intends to visit France when he is able. He has a great affection for our country, and during the war disinterestedly gave his support to pro-Allied propaganda and later to American patriotic services. In this last connection he undertook a great tour promoting Liberty Bonds and achieved remarkable results. This was hardly surprising, considering his popularity in the United States. When his propaganda tour was over, he resumed production. We can await his new films with confidence, as worthy successors to the unforgettable Mutual series of twelve films, which I saw in America, and of which the first have already been released in France.

'I have seen certain writers speaking a little disdainfully of Charlie. As if the fact of making his fellow men laugh by wholesome means and a real psychological study deserved a sort of scorn. As for those who do not find him funny, I don't know whether they have seen him at all; but for certain, they constitute only an infinitesimal minority among the public. Those who do not like him either do not know him properly, or confuse him with feeble imitators. Can there really be any doubt of the pains that must be taken to make one's fellow-men laugh, and is it not particularly unjust to us to pour scorn on us because we try to distract for a few moments the vast public that frequents the cinemas? Is not laughter one of man's greatest gifts? Is it not indispensable to our moral health and equilibrium?

'What nonsense to say that Charlie or others only make people laugh by cutting capers. It is impossible to make people laugh merely with capers: they must be cut comically. Occasionally a laugh may be obtained in a theatre or music hall by an instinctive natural effect, and a gift for that may be enough to make a successful actor. But in the cinema that is virtually impossible, for there it is only possible to show off natural gifts with a degree of preparation and an intelligent labour that is not adequately appreciated. What instinct can discover, it is necessary to translate into this special language, reducing the effects to their elements, in mathematically calculating their results, in controlling their exposition point by point. Those who imitate Chaplin accomplish perfectly the same tricks or gags as he does. Why then do they not inspire the same laughter? And let those who scoff try some of those "capers" in front of a camera lens. They will see then if it is the same thing. We are reproached, again, obliquely, for earning millions. Do they think that the people who pay us are making a bad bargain, and that they are cheated by us? We earn this money by making people laugh, if we are capable of it. A man like Chaplin makes the half of all humanity laugh, several times a year.

'Do you believe that that does not deserve a few millions?'

'In any event, the public has already adequately answered the criticisms which can be made on this subject. The public is our sovereign judge, and I believe sincerely that it is the public alone which has the power to build up these great cinematographic reputations. Charlie's is sufficiently established for there to be no need to justify it. It deserves only to be studied, and commentated. Is it not the most convincing proof of the value in film production of backing extraordinary talent with order and system and hard work?

'Charlie Chaplin, director and actor, is in my opinion a perfect model for all those who, wishing to create cinema, will have to study and understand. To imitate is a proof of inferiority and impotence. Chaplin has a particular costume. He has made his physique, his gait, his own genre famous. All this may be stolen from him. It is a pointless theft. But to trace the reasons for his success, to extract from them formulas and complex indications, that is to learn one's job in the finest school. I will be pardoned for speaking of Charlie Chaplin with such warmth. Before knowing him I was only his greatest admirer. Today, I am his friend ...'

Another artist who in the different area of direction can be regarded as Chaplin's peer recorded his admiration in a long essay. Just after the Second World War the great Soviet director Sergei Eisenstein undertook to edit a series of books, to be published in the Soviet Union, on the history of world cinema. His unfortunate decision to devote the first two volumes to the American film were to be used with great malevolence against him in the years when Stalinist policy condemned 'cosmopolitanism', and contributed greatly to the official disfavour which clouded and oppressed the last years of this greatest of Soviet artists.

Eisenstein's was one of the four essays in the book – the others were by the critic M. Bleiman and the directors Serge Yutkevitch and Grigori Kozintsev. Eisenstein appears to have written his contribution in Alma Ata, at the height of the war in 1943–1944. It runs to some ten thousand words

Chaplin with Sergei M. Eisenstein. Photographed by Grigori Alexandrov in Hollywood, 1930.

and is entitled 'Charlie the Kid': 'I think that this combination of Chaplin's name and the title of one of the most popular of his films, is worthy of being used to identify its creator; the appellation reveals his inner nature, just as "Conqueror", "Coeur de Lion" and "Terrible" describe the natures of William of Normandy, of the legendary Richard and the wise Tsar Ivan IV of Muscovy.'

The essay is a characteristically brilliant combination of wit, fantasy, erudition and an extraordinary richness of allusion. What thrills him, Eisenstein says, and what he wants to understand in Chaplin is not direction, methods, tricks, the technique of his humour. 'When I think of Chaplin I want, first of all, to penetrate that strange system of thinking which perceives phenomena in such a strange way and responds to them with such strange images. I would like to penetrate that part of this system of thinking which, before it becomes an outlook of life, exists in the stage of contemplation of the environment.'

'What do those unusual eyes – Chaplin's eyes – see?' he asks. A primary characteristic of Chaplin, says Eisenstein, is that he has preserved the outlook and spontaneous reactions of a child. Hence his freedom from the ordinary fetters of morals and his ability to see as comic things which make other peoples' flesh creep. This leads him into a remarkable digression upon infant-ilism as a basis of American comedy, comparing it with Victorian England's delight in nonsense. He quotes an American psychologist of the twenties, (H. A. Overstreet, in *Influencing Human Behaviour*): 'To imply ... that a per-son has a fine sense of humour is to imply that he has still in him the spirit of play, which implies even more deeply the spirit of freedom and of creative spontaneity.' At this point Eisenstein recalls his sense of Marxist-Stalinist duty, and reflects that phrases like 'Escape from reality', 'Relapse to child-hood' and 'infantilism' do not find much favour in the Soviet Union. 'At our end of the world we do not escape from reality to fairy tale; we make fairy tales real.

'Our task is not to plunge adults into childhood but to make the children's paradise of the past accessible to every grown-up in every citizen of the Soviet Union.'

Even the great Eisenstein, at this uneasy time in history, was obliged to torture his arguments in order to accommodate both his social obligations and his undoubted adoration of Chaplin:

'That is why Chaplin's genius was born and developed at the other end of the world and not in a country where everything has been done to make the golden paradise of childhood a reality.

'That is why his genius was bound to shine in a country where the method and type of his humour was a necessity, where the realization of a childish dream by a grown-up man comes up against insurmountable obstacles.'

Eisenstein then passes to the moral implications of the infantile view. 'To be able to perceive the image of things spontaneously and quickly – without their moral and ethical interpretation, without speculating or passing his judgment on them, just as a laughing child sees them – that is what dis-tinguishes Chaplin, makes him unique and inimitable.

'The spontaneousness of seeing engenders the perception of the ridiculous and the perception overgrows into a conception.'

But the conception has three aspects. When the event itself is quite harm-less, Chaplin's perception clothes it in 'inimitable buffoonery'. When the event is 'dramatic in a personal way' – that is, sentimental or pathetic, Chaplin's perception 'gives rise to a humorous melodrama of the best specimens of his individual style in which smiles are mixed with tears'. But when the event is tragic in a social way, 'it is no longer a child's toy, no longer a problem for a child's mind, and the humorously childish look gives rise to a series of horrible scenes in *Modern Times*'.

Eisenstein's remarks help to explain the poor reception of *Modern Times* on its first release in the Soviet Union, which gravely puzzled Chaplin and his contemporaries: '*Modern Times* has undoubtedly revealed the "secret of his eyes". So long as his splendid comedies dealt with conflicts between good and bad people, small and big, who, as if by accident, were at the same

Chaplin (*left*) *as Napoleon – a role which long fascinated him. His admirer and fellow-comedian Jerry Lewis also tried the imperial costume* (*right*).

92

time divided into the rich and poor, his eyes laughed or cried, depending on his theme. But when in the years of American depression the good and bad personages suddenly turned out to be real representatives of antagonist social groups, Chaplin's eyes began to blink, then closed, and then stubbornly fixed themselves on the modern times and *new* phenomena, regarding them *in the old way*, and in this he began to contradict his theme.

'This made the style of his films uneven, led to the monstrous and revolting treatment of the theme, and completely revealed the secret of Chaplin's eyes.'

Eisenstein, revealing that his notes on Chaplin were first started in 1937, at the time of the Soviet première of *Modern Times*, goes on to elaborate his notion of Chaplin's infantilism, comparing it with the nature of the actual child's view of the world. With *The Great Dictator*, though, he declares, Chaplin arrived at maturity. 'In this film Chaplin's "infantile method" of looking at life and making comedies became the salient feature of the character of a live man (if the prototype of Adenoid Hynkel *can* be called a man) and of the actual methods of governing a real country.

'Chaplin's method of producing comic effects, which always triumphed over the means of his infantile approach to phenomena, was transplanted into the characterization of the protagonist in *The Dictator* ...'

'And today –', continued Eisenstein, passing into the eccentric style he adopted to give emphasis to his notions.

'it is Charlie

'it is Chaplin,

'who,

'by one method or other,

'by some means or other,

'looking at life with his childishly naive and *childishly wise* eyes,

'creates in *The Dictator* an impressive and devastating satire glorifying the Triumph of the Human Mind over Bestiality.

'Thereby Chaplin takes his place in the ranks of the great masters who throughout the ages, have been fighting Darkness with the weapon of Satire ...'

The last word, perhaps, should be with a more modern artist and a fellow comedian. Jerry Lewis, who elsewhere in his book *The Total Film-Maker* calls Chaplin 'this beautiful little man', wrote: 'I am convinced that the best example of a total film-maker was Chaplin. He was totally in, on and all over his films. He created them in the fullest sense of the word, experimented to see how widely, how cleverly and skilfully he could work.'

Opinion of the Thirties

At the start of the thirties, no-one ever questioned that Chaplin was the greatest figure in the movies. Indeed he was the most famous and best-loved man in the world. He was rich and fêted by the great of all nations. He was unmarried; and his name was romantically linked by the popular press with a succession of some of the most glamorous and desirable women in the world. Yet this decade was to bring him much anxiety and a sense of insecurity in his creative work. There was, above all, the looming ogre of sound. By the time that *The Circus* was released talking pictures were a fact of Hollywood life. Throughout the thirties Chaplin was to agonize and temporize over how he must alter and perhaps compromise his art, developed through and intrinsic to the silent screen, to suit the new technology.

The times had changed; and so in a different way, according to his critics, had Chaplin. The humanist sentiment which was part of his temperament and integral to his work almost from the beginning, had become more and more overt. Chaplin began to face the criticism that the clown had strayed outside his proper field, and was seeking to turn philosopher and commentator on his times. Other signs were more ominous. From the start reactionary America had identified Chaplin's idiosyncratic, generous humanism as Bolshevism. Chaplin's first English biographer (no very reliable witness, as we shall discover) wrote cheerfully in 1931, 'Charlie Chaplin may or may not hold revolutionary views on politics. Some newspaper men believe that he is a Bolshevik, but beyond the fact that he has made a fortune out of the sale of his pictures in Russia, there is not the slightest warrant for the suggestion'. (For that matter, there was no warrant for the suggestion that Chaplin had made any money out of Russia.)

Jan and Cora Gordon, journalists and artists, writing in 1930 in their *Stardust in Hollywood* were shrewder prophets and commentators on the fickle character of the American public. The Gordons commented upon the world-wide popularity of Chaplin, instancing the example of a friend who had exhibited Chaplin films to sometimes over-enthusiastic audiences in Lagos. 'In the hearts of almost every race, no matter whether it is European, Oriental, African, Celestial or Esquimo, the genius of Charlie has been recognized and is welcomed. Only in America, from which the greater part of his humour has been drawn, is Charlie looked on with a rather dubious face.

'This does not mean that in the States the films of Charlie are not packed, nor that the intellectuals refuse him the film pre-eminence that he is accorded by all the intellectuals of Europe. The children and the poor ensure his overwhelming success. But the *bourgeoisie* instinctively repudiate him. He stands for something that denies the whole of their collective philosophy. He proclaims the importance of subtle spiritual values that may lie behind failure, and he creates poems of humour praising the resilience of the feckless.

'The members of the great *bourgeoisie* may be amused at Charlie in spite of themselves, but there is something in him repugnant to them. Thus, the newspapers and the self-righteous fall like wolves on his unfortunate matrimonial experiences. In fact – Charlie being above the ordinary processes of the Black List – we heard one leading club woman exclaim:

'"That Charlie Chaplin, he's got to look after himself. I tell you that if he has one more scandal the whole of the women's clubs of America are going to combine against him. We shall issue a boycott against his films, and any cinema house that dares to show him will be ostracized. Then you'll see what your great Mr Chaplin looks like. He just can't outrage the great American public too far."'

Sad to say the Gordons, with their very lively response to all they saw in Hollywood, never managed to meet Chaplin. They had permission to sketch on the sets of *City Lights*, but the production was postponed; and they were shrewd enough to avoid casual meetings: 'His star-meeting-the-public manner,' they speculated, 'should be a masterpiece of polite camouflage.'

If Chaplin had serious misgivings about the threat of sound to his essentially mimic art (and it appears that the production of *City Lights* was delayed to allow him a period of reflection on the problem) he did not acknowledge them in retrospect. 'I was a pantomimist and in that medium I was unique and, without false modesty, a master.' The arguments against introducing dialogue into films were commercial as well as artistic. Pantomime – particularly Chaplin's pantomime – was a universal language: English dialogue would seriously restrict a market which till this time had been universal. (Chaplin always reckoned to earn back his production costs from Japan alone.)

A few critics were delighted to charge Chaplin with reactionary cowardice; but most writers of the time had neither difficulty in understanding his situation nor desire to see him change. The author of an early study of sound film techniques and aesthetics, John Scotland, writing in 1930, specifically excluded Chaplin from the debate: 'Chaplin, of course, resides in a motion picture class of his own. He is probably the one artist in the whole of the motion-picture industry who can stand out against "Talkies" and still remain as popular as ever as the perfect mime. He dislikes "Talkies" immensely, seeing in them nothing but a menace to motion-picture art. From his own point of view he is absolutely right, because one gesture from him tells more than five minutes of dialogue would, but then he is the outstanding genius which the motion-picture has produced, and has a grip of the medium in which he works such as has not been attained by any other man.'

So Chaplin conceived and made *City Lights* in the way he had always worked, as a silent film. The essential story of the little tramp who falls in love with a beautiful blind girl, struggles against all odds to raise money to cure her, and must then face the dreadful moment when she sees the unbecoming form of her benefactor, is the sort of old-style melodrama which often formed an effective pathetic basis to his comedies.

With the intervals for reflection *City Lights* was three years in the making. By the time it was ready for release, in 1931, it was clear that it must at least have a musical accompaniment; and so for the first time Chaplin applied his talents as a composer of musical accompaniment. The style of his musical scores, very much derived from the techniques of incidental music in the nineteenth century theatre, with its use of leitmotifs and direct pointing of the action (known in pictures as 'mickey-mousing' because of the similarity to the technique of fitting action and music in animated films) ideally suits his visual style.

Chaplin was confident enough about his rejection of dialogue to kid the talkies a little in the film. The opening scene shows a large crowd assembled for the unveiling of a statue representing 'Peace and Prosperity'. The speeches of the dignitaries officiating at the ceremony are represented by grotesque gabble produced by saxophones. When the veil falls from the statue, Prosperity is seen to be cradling the wretched figure of the tramp. As he tries to make his escape from the angry assembly, he is hooked by the seat of his pants on the sword of the figure presumably – ironically – representing peace.

Later in the day, after a series of mishaps with police, insolent newsboys and a trapdoor in the pavement, he comes upon the blind flower-girl. The meeting provides a telling example of his juxtaposition of pathos and farce: The radiant Charlie sits silently contemplating the sad and lovely girl. She, with wonderful grace, takes her flower bucket and throws away the dirty water – directly over the unseen Charlie.

That night Charlie prevents a drunken millionaire from throwing himself into the river; and almost gets drowned himself for his pains. Later he comes near to being shot in another of the erratic millionaire's suicide attempts; but afterwards the elated new friend takes Charlie out for a night on the town and concludes an evening rich in comic interludes by giving Charlie his Rolls Royce, as well as money for the poor flower-girl.

The next day, sober and unfriendly, the millionaire has no recollection of the night before, or of Charlie, and has him thrown out of the house. The pattern is repeated that night. The millionaire meets Charlie, greets him as a cherished friend and takes him to a party, which provides opportunities

City Lights *1931. Chaplin with Harry Myers as the alcoholic millionaire.*

for more comic embarrassments. The next morning, finding Charlie in bed beside him, the sobered millionaire angrily orders out the apparent stranger.

Finding the flower girl is not at her place on the street corner, Charlie goes to the garret where she lives with her grandmother; and finds that she is ill and in need of special care. To earn some money to help her, Charlie works as a street cleaner, and takes part in a boxing match which proves disastrous – but is one of Chaplin's greatest pieces of comic choreography (it took a month to rehearse).

Luckily he again meets the millionaire, in a state of amiable inebriation. He gives Charlie the money; but after a contretemps with some burglars and the millionaire's return to sober hostility, Charlie is suspected of robbery. He is arrested and gaoled; but not before he has passed over to the blind girl the money which will take her to Europe for the operation that will restore her sight.

Months later, Charlie, more wretched than ever after his release from gaol, passes a flower shop, in which the girl and her grandmother are now established. The girl, looking out of the window in constant hope of seeing her benefactor, whom she has imagined as rich and handsome, takes pity on this sad little tramp. She proffers a coin; but he hurries off, embarrassed. She follows and presses the coin into his hand. She recognizes him by touch and asks, incredulously (a title, of course) 'You?'. He nods; (title) 'You can see now?' (title) 'Yes. I can see now.' Of the look that Chaplin returns to her – proud, ashamed, timid, hopeful, enigmatic – the critic James Agee wrote 'it is the greatest piece of acting and the highest moment in movies'. On its West Coast release, public reaction to the film was tepid; but when it opened in New York – where Chaplin acted as his own distributor since United Artists were not prepared to meet his financial terms – it proved a huge commercial success.

Chaplin then embarked upon a trip round the world, partly to promote *City Lights*. In the course of it he was much struck by the effects of world-wide depression, and began to formulate his own economic theories. His impromptu lectures to European politicians were received, as Chaplin's biographer Theodore Huff says rather patronizingly, 'good-naturedly'. Einstein, however, complimented him, 'You're not a comedian. You are an economist.' A variety of social and industrial impressions, not excluding his own childhood memories of social institutions and of minding a printing machine which dwarfed him, in one of his earliest spells of employment, combined to give

Chaplin with Paulette Goddard, about 1935.

him the idea for *Modern Times*. Further inspiration for the female lead, whom Chaplin named the 'gamin' and who had more vitality and independence than any Chaplin heroine since Mabel Normand, was provided by his encounter with Paulette Goddard. The two were introduced aboard Joseph Schenck's yacht: Goddard, born Pauline Levy in New York in 1911, was then under contract to Hal Roach.

Modern Times *1936.*

Modern Times was the most elaborate production Chaplin had undertaken, involving the building of two vast sets, one the factory where we first discover Charlie as a production worker; the other a five-acre city section where most of the remaining action was located.

The opening title of the film rather overstates the case in calling it 'The story of industry, of individual enterprise – humanity crusading in the pursuit of happiness.' The film begins with a satirical stroke – a shot of sheep running is juxtaposed with scenes of workers crowding out of a subway. Charlie's job on the factory production line is to tighten up two bolts on each of an endless succession of components for who knows what mysterious product. When he misses a move, because of the attentions of a wasp, the whole production line is thrown into chaos. Later he is used as a guinea pig to try out an automatic feeding machine, designed to save money by feeding workers at the production line. The machine runs amok and destroys itself, with considerable indignity and mess for Charlie.

Finally driven berserk by the production line, Charlie dances out into the street, tightening everything in sight including the buttons on a large lady's bodice. In a state of nervous breakdown he is placed in hospital; but on release is quickly in trouble again. Helpfully running after a truck to return a red warning flag which has fallen from it, a line of demonstrating workers take him for their leader and form up behind him. Thrown into gaol he accidentally frustrates a gaol break. Pardon and release is no reward however, since he is once again thrown out into a cold, unfriendly world.

He meets Paulette, whose father has been shot in a labour battle, and who is being pursued by juvenile care officers (never a benevolent force in Chaplin films). She is apprehended; and Charlie endeavours to get himself arrested in order to return to the more homely world of prison. When they meet in a patrol wagon, however, he and Paulette are inspired to escape. They share daydreams of cosy domesticity, though the reality of their waterside shack and Charlie's job as a nightwatchman in a department store is less picturesque. Charlie again lands in gaol when the department store is robbed by some of his former prison companions.

Meanwhile Paulette has found a job singing in a cafe; and on Charlie's release persuades the owner to give him a job as a waiter. After a fine series of comic variations on the difficulties of carrying a roast duck across a crowded dance floor, Charlie is suddenly called upon to take the place of the cabaret singer.

This was the historic moment at which Chaplin's voice was heard from the screen. It was also the last appearance of the tramp, except for the traces that still remain in the little Jewish barber in *The Great Dictator*. Even now Chaplin managed to avoid conventional dialogue. Charlie, the waiter, is nervous that he will not remember the words of the song, so Paulette writes them on his starched, detachable cuffs. The cuffs prove all too detachable, and fly away through the air at his first expansive gesture. So, without words, he concocts a marvellous improvisation of gibberish, with a vaguely

Modern Times *1936. Charlie has just taken the blame for stealing a loaf, to save Paulette Goddard from prison.*

Franco-Italian inflection, to the tune of *Titine*.

The applause for the performance is cut short by the arrival of the juvenile care officers. Charlie and Paulette make a brisk escape and are last seen walking off down a dirt road and into the sun, hand in hand.

*   *   *

About the time that *City Lights* was released, the first biography of Chaplin in book form appeared in English – discounting the unauthorized and suppressed *Charlie Chaplin's Own Story* of 1916. *Charlie Chaplin His Life and Art* was by William Dodgson Bowman (on the title page of the book he appears as 'Wm Dodgson Bowman') whose principal literary effort it seems to have been, and was first published in London by George Routledge and Sons and in Toronto by the Musson Book Company. It is mentioned by none of Chaplin's subsequent biographers, nor by Chaplin's own *Autobiography*, not surprisingly perhaps, since it is not impressively accurate or revealing. Nevertheless when it was published in the United States by the John Day Company, Douglas Fairbanks was prevailed upon to provide an introduction; and in 1974 the original London edition (without the Fairbanks introduction) was reprinted as part of an 'American Biographies' series.

Bowman's information was mainly gleaned from Chaplin's own 1921 book *My Trip Abroad* (in England, *My Wonderful Visit*) and from articles in fan magazines; but introduces such disconcerting pieces of misinformation as that 'His first photo play was *Tillie's Punctured Romance*'. The critical stance is the idolatrous awe of genius that characterized most twenties writing. 'The end is not yet', he says; 'To outward seeming Charlie Chaplin has reached the summit of his ambitions. Fortune has poured into his lap every gift that the heart of man can desire. But he would be rash who could declare that for this great artist, still at the zenith of his powers, there are no more summits to achieve, no more worlds to conquer. Is it improbable that in his musings he may yet have glimpses of the light that never was on sea or land, and so present the world with a masterpiece that will be prized as a treasure beyond price?' Wm Dodgson Bowman had a lyrical turn to his prose.

The freshest part of the book is a little tail-piece 'Charlie and the Talkies' which was evidently added as an afterthought to bring the text up to date with *City Lights*. In matters of art, Mr Bowman charges, Chaplin is a die-hard conservative. Alone he has stood out against the revolution of the past three years, feeling, as Chaplin himself said, 'like the boy on the burning deck whence all but he had fled'. Chaplin himself, he says, has admitted that good work is being done with the talkies; but some of it is most distressing. Much is being said in sound films that would be better left unsaid; the strong silent men no longer seem so strong when they are not silent; and many pretty young actresses would have been better seen and not heard. 'Some complain that the microphone fails to do justice to their voices, though they know that it is not justice but mercy they want.'

Bowman says that facts confirm Chaplin's judgment that sound must destroy the universal language of pantomime. 'The talkie invasion has caused much confusion and discord. In Prague, a German dialogue film was shouted down simply because it was German. The people of Budapest have threatened similar action. Audiences in Paris have in one case refused to listen to the American dialogue of a Hollywood film, and in another to the German accent of a player in a French talkie. Picture-goers in some parts of South America obstinately object to talkies in Castilian Spanish.'

Chaplin, says Bowman, as his parting shot on the subject, is unimpressed by the fact that Bernard Shaw believes in talkies; and indeed questions Shaw's prophecy in predicting the death of the theatre. 'Shaw,' says Chaplin, according to Bowman, 'is a great actor himself ... He is more attached to his makeup than I am to mine. At least I don't take my moustache to bed with me.'

For all its inadequacies, Bowman's *Charlie Chaplin* was to remain for nine years the only English-language biography of the film maker. In France the decade saw the publication of two more studies, Philippe Soupault's *Charlot* (1931) and Pierre Leprohon's *Charlot, ou la Naissance d'un Mythe* (1935). In addition two slightly scandalous volumes of personal memoirs, appeared in French editions: *Le Vérité sur Charlie Chaplin* by Chaplin's erstwhile press secretary, Carlyle T. Robinson; and *Charlie Chaplin Intime* by May Reeves whose intimacy with Chaplin had in fact been responsible for the sacking of Robinson. The first Spanish life of Chaplin, *El genio del septimo arte: Apologia de Charlot*, by Santiago Aguila, appeared in 1930.

The daily and periodical press remained as loyal to Chaplin as ever. On both sides of the Atlantic *City Lights* received enthusiastic reviews. Chaplin's conservatism on the matter of sound seemed actually to be welcomed: talking pictures, everyone agreed, had been a mixed blessing.

In *The Bookman*, Francis Fergusson, one of the best dramatic critics of the period, justified himself in discussing the film in a column devoted to the stage, since Chaplin's method 'provides a model many stage artists would do well to study'. For Fergusson, Chaplin's decision to eschew sound is a positive merit in the film: 'It is lucky for us all that he developed as a speechless clown, and that he was wise enough to not make his new film "talkie". He never tells us about anything, he shows us something, and we laugh or cry. Words are hard even for a poet to bring to life, and a writer of dialogue can hardly hope to attain anything like the immediacy of a good image, much less of an authentic moment of acting.'

Fergusson goes on to praise the 'ironic gleam' of the final scenes of the film, 'like Chaplin stepping from behind the tramp make-up, and confessing he knew from the first what a sinister business life was'. He sees a similar sense of the cruelty of life in comic mishaps like the tramp's fall into the harbour while trying to prevent the millionaire from killing himself; and a scene where Charlie, having played an exquisite series of variations with an open trapdoor, which is always fortuitously closed by an elevator whenever he steps on it, finally falls in. Fergusson in his admiration readily forgives inadequacies in the surrounding context of scenery and supporting players. 'Chaplin's poetry is confined to the character of Charlie Chaplin the hobo and his adventures. This figure moves, like Don Quixote in Kansas City, against an accurately photographed background of prize-fighters, rich men and snappy street crowds such as we see daily.'

A dissenting view of *City Lights* appeared in an extremely lively volume of essays which appeared in 1931 under the title *Star Gazing*. Its author, June Head, described it as 'an entirely unprejudiced and low-brow book'. Her admiration for Chaplin is beyond doubt. She approves his 'infinite wisdom' in not going talkie; and values the character he created so far as to speculate that if Chaplin chose to work out Charlie's destiny in some 'conclusive masterpiece of screen art' he might become as immortal in his own sphere as Shakespeare.

Yet *City Lights* as a whole, much as she admires individual parts, does not, she feels, do justice to his talents. 'Had it been shown anonymously, I doubt whether the film would have had anything but the coldest reception. It consisted simply of a series of knockabout incidents strung on a frail thread of sentimentality. The humour was good, satisfying, old-fashioned slapstick, and the audience loved it because it gets so little of that kind of fun nowadays ...

'It was the weakness of the sentiment which should have joined those episodes into a decisive pattern, but failed to do so, that marked a departure from the former Chaplin standard ...

'At the risk of rousing a chorus of enraged howls from his admirers, I would suggest that what Chaplin needs is a really good producer. Chaplin's own production methods are those of ten years ago. His finished film is rough and uneven, badly photographed, the decor is often actively offensive, his leading ladies uninteresting, and the continuity leaves much to be desired ... *City Lights* took between two and three years to make, a period out of all proportion to the result achieved.'

With *Modern Times* the spectrum of critical opinion broadened; and the partisanship which was to grow amongst writers on Chaplin first became evident. The shades of opinion on *Modern Times* are most vividly demonstrated in the concluding section of *Garbo and the Night Watchman*, a classic anthology of critical writing on films collected in 1937 by Alistair Cooke, and reprinted in 1971 by Secker and Warburg. The rest of the book had consisted of selected reviews by a group of nine chosen critics. The final section collected together what each of these critics had written on a single film, *Modern Times*. The reason for this arrangement, the editor explained, was that *Modern Times* was the ranking box-office film of its year and had probably been seen by more readers than any other film mentioned in the book. Moreover, he said, the character was the most famous in screen history; and 'whatever doubts a critic has to resolve, Charlie Chaplin is not one of them'.

Robert Herring, an English critic of wide interests and a complex and elusive literary style confessed to holding no special brief for Chaplin, but expressed a preference for this film over *The Circus* and *City Lights*. There is, he said, plenty of loose thinking in the film; but Chaplin 'like most of those who write most about the film', is not a thinker; and in his better moments does not set out to be. Herring lists some of these moments in the film, admiring it mostly for Chaplin's ability to rag our fears.

The American Don Herold, himself a professional humorist, dismissed as 'bunk' the idea that Chaplin, at least in his pictures, was a deep-searching, penetrating philosopher or a subtle sociological observer and satirist. For Herold he was much more – a comic genius, 'and it all adds up into humorous beauty, into ballet art at its highest and best'.

For the rest the opinions were fairly clearly split. One party, while

Modern Times *1936. Chaplin and Paulette Goddard.*

acknowledging that Chaplin himself was still the most subtle and comic of all pantomime artists felt that as a film maker he had been overtaken by time, and that his attempts to reflect upon the modern world were, conversely, misguided. John Marks in the London *New Statesman and Nation* felt the very title of the film was a misnomer, that Chaplin's pathos had overtaken him, that the film was ten years behind the times, and that the silent techniques and use of titles slowed up the film hopelessly. The 'ballet movements', he acknowledged, had a psychological significance from time to time; but the film was far less funny than *City Lights*. Meyer Levin, the artist and novelist, then working as film critic for *Esquire*, was more generous. Yet even he, while admiring the eating machine sequence as 'the greatest satiric commentary on mechanized civilization' he had ever encountered, saw the film as a kind of anthology, a collected complete edition of Chaplin's earlier work; and hoped that the reception of the film would once and for all prove to the comedian that he could have adopted modern techniques – 'could have kept all of his stylistic simplicities without adhering to the crudities, such as the often unnecessary sub-titles'.

The least merciful of the critics of the time was Otis Ferguson, then film critic of *The New Republic*, though he also wrote criticism of high calibre on literature, theatre and jazz. (He was killed in action in 1943, at the age of 36.) Chaplin himself, he admitted, was not dated, and never would be: 'he is a reservoir of humour, master of an infinite array of dodges, agile in both mind and body. He is not only a character but a complete character, with the perfect ability to make evident all the shades of his odd and charming feelings; not only a touching character, but a first-class buffoon and I guess the master of our time in dumb show. But this does not make him a first-class picture maker'. *Modern Times*, he quipped, was the last thing they should have called it: its times were modern many years before, when the movies were young. The antiquity of the sets, the characters, the handling of performers and groups irked him; and, with some justice, he pointed out that the film really takes the form of several one- or two-reelers for which he proposes as suitable titles, *The Shop*, *The Jailbird*, *The Watchman*, *The Singing Waiter*.

Ferguson kept to the end of his article the supreme damnation of faint praise: 'on the screen he is only partly a citizen of this world: he lives mostly in that unreal happy land – you see the little figure walking off down the road toward it always into the fade-out – where kicks, thumps, injustice and nowhere to sleep are no more than a teasing and a jolly dream (Oh, with a little pang perhaps, a gentle Woollcott tear) and the stuff a paying public's cherished happy endings are made of'. (Throughout the twenties and thirties Alexander Woollcott's somewhat lachrymose dedication to Chaplin in his more sentimental aspects was a standing joke with the sophisticated critics.)

Alistair Cooke, as editor of this sequence of reviews, headed his article with a quotation from a *Fortune* article on the Modern Interior: 'Streamlining a water closet cuts neither wind resistance nor ice and has nothing to do with the science of aerodynamics'. While on one hand he felt that Chaplin, with his subtitles, was partly stuck in the past, and that '*Modern Times* is never once on the plane of social satire', he regretted that in other respects Chaplin had too much 'modernised' himself. '*Modern Times* is like Chaplin the actor directed and produced by MGM.' He instanced the realistic decors, the polished photography (Cartier Bresson had preferred Chaplin's 'bad' photography to the banal excellences of modern Hollywood films), and the lush score orchestrated by Alfred Newman (in fact Newman had left the film in exasperation at Chaplin's demands). Cooke nevertheless rejoiced that 'Chaplin has kept his promise that he was about to extinguish Everybody's Little Ray of Sunshine. The tragic comedian is no more.' The tramp in this film is a good deal more resilient and perky and cheeky to cops than the more submissive little man of *City Lights*. In large part, several critics felt, this was because in Paulette Goddard Chaplin had a much more spirited and unsentimental leading lady than he had played against for more than twenty years. Inevitably Paulette Goddard was singled out by the admirable Cecelia Ager, an early feminist.

Two critics in the *Garbo and the Night Watchmen* groups were unequivocal in their admiration of *Modern Times*. Kyle Crichton (1896–1960), writing under the name Robert Forsythe, which he used for his more aggressive political writings, called *Modern Times* 'not so much a fine motion picture as a historical event'. Crichton, born of working class Scottish parents in industrial Pennsylvania, had like Chaplin memories of an underprivileged childhood and the realities of the streets. 'For the first time,' he wrote, 'an American film was daring to challenge the superiority of an industrial civilization based upon the creed of men who sit at flat-topped desks and press buttons demanding more speed from tortured employees.

Celebrity: *Chaplin with Bernard Shaw, London 1931.*

There were cops beating demonstrators and shooting down the unemployed (specifically the father of the waif who is later picked up by Chaplin), there is a belt line which operates at such a pace that men go insane, there is a heart-breaking scene of the helpless couple trying to squeeze out happiness in a little home of their own (a shack in a Hooverville colony). It is the story of a pathetic little man trying bravely to hold up his end in this mad world.'

'Chaplin's methods,' continues Crichton/Forsythe, 'are too kindly for great satire, but by the very implication of the facts with which he deals he has created a biting commentary upon our civilization. He has made high humour out of material which is fundamentally tragic.'

Forsythe the radical exults that, with the distributive machinery of the movies in the hands of the most reactionary forces in the country, Chaplin has nevertheless succeeded in making an honest picture in Hollywood. He provides a touching epigraph: 'It is a triumph not only of his art but of his heart. What his political views are, I don't know and don't care. He has the feelings of an honest man and that is enough.'

For Graham Greene, then film critic of *The Spectator*, 'the little man has at last definitely entered the contemporary scene'. Greene seemed to come much nearer than the rest to the point, when he declared that there was no political passion in the film, that it was a good deal less and a good deal more than socialist in intention, that there is certainly no indication that the little man would be any more at home at Dniepostroi. Chaplin, he said, was an artist and not a propagandist. He does not try to explain; all he does is to present, 'with vivid fantasy what seems to him a crazy comic tragic world without a plan, ... He presents, he doesn't offer political solutions'.

Father and Sons

It is not to be wondered at if Chaplin, who as a child had been deprived
of a normal stable home life, should seem all his years to have been in quest
of a conventional, comfortable domestic existence, surrounded by a family.
Ironically the desire was to remain frustrated and unsatisfied until a comparatively late period of the artist's life. He was fifty-four before he married
Oona O'Neill who was finally to give him a large family, and the domestic
contentment which was to endure for almost thirty years, until his death.

Chaplin's first marriage to Mildred Harris quickly failed: Miss Harris felt
that their relationship became impossible after the death in infancy of their
only child. His second marriage to Lita Gray gave him two sons; but the
union was clearly doomed almost from the start by the incompatibility of
the partners. Chaplin and his third wife, Paulette Goddard, were clearly better
suited both intellectually and temperamentally; but the marriage was child-
less; and as independent artists they eventually went their own ways. According to his son, Charles Chaplin Junior, Chaplin once said, 'I am not so sure
that I should ever marry. I like to be free to travel; free to eat at any time
and free to do as I please. When I work I am oblivious to the world and
it's difficult to ask any woman to be happy when at times I forget her very
existence.' As his son, Charles Junior had become 'familiar with that strange,
inwardly directed concentration which had made life so difficult and lonely
for Mildred Harris and my mother. Now when we came home from school
Dad would be down in the living room ostensibly to greet us. But ten to
one some idea would have caught him just before we came in and he would
be sitting at his table working.'

Charles Chaplin Junior was the elder of Chaplin's two sons by Lita (or
Lillita) Gray. He was born in May or June 1925: his mother told him that
the record of his birth had been falsified (changing the date from May 5
to June 28) so as not to provide cause for scandal to persons of the twenties
with calculating minds – Chaplin and Lita had married only in November
1924. Young Charles himself had a brief unsuccessful marriage, and died
in 1968.

He was educated (strangely, considering his father's powerful feelings
about militarism) at the Black-Foxe Military Academy in Hollywood, and

Limelight: *Charles Chaplin with his son, Sydney Chaplin as the young composer.*

saw service in the Second World War. After a spell in the dramatic department of U.C.L.A. he began his acting career at the Circle Theater in Hollywood, a progressive little theatre group established by his younger brother Sydney, Jerry Epstein, who was later to become a close associate of their father, and other friends. The only significant memorial of Charles Junior's brief career is his appearance as a comic policeman in the pantomime sequence of *Limelight*.

In 1960 Charles Chaplin Junior published a memoir, *My Father, Charles Chaplin*, written with the collaboration of two highly professional and sympathetic Hollywood journalists N. and M. Rau. Chaplin himself, it is reasonable to guess, would not have been overjoyed at this family revelation; as his son comments, 'Dad ... craves privacy more than any other man I know.' Nevertheless he would have had little cause for real displeasure. This is as affectionate and understanding a tribute as any father might hope for. Even allowing for the collaboration of other writers, young Charles does emerge clearly defined as a person of warmth and generosity. In his dedication, 'Memo to my father', he quotes Chaplin's own reflections, in *My Trip Abroad*, upon Lord Birkenhead's intention to write a life of his father, the jurist and statesman the Earl of Birkenhead: 'This was quite a task, I thought, and wondered if a son, in doing such a biography, could sufficiently detach himself from the subject so as to see the deep shadows as well as the highlights which are necessary to a true portrait of a great man.' 'Since this book will come as a surprise to you, I hope I have achieved that detachment you questioned of Lord Birkenhead. As for your being a great man, I have found that even your rankest enemies concede that in your realm of talent you have no peer. Respectfully, Your son, Charles.'

In such a case detachment cannot have been easily achieved. When Charles Junior was still a baby his parents had divorced in a case surrounded by lurid publicity and acrimony on both sides. Since the divorce there had more than once been legal proceedings relating to the two children, which had only served to aggravate the hostility between the former husband and wife. Charles and Sydney had been given into custody of their mother, although they were mostly brought up by their grandmother, since Lita had established a career for herself as a singer, and was often absent from home. As the boys grew older, they frequently visited their father for weekends and for longer spells. Throughout his recollections of childhood and adolescence, the son is scrupulous in his loyalty to both parents, refusing absolutely to apportion any favour or blame. With wistful eagerness he clings to the moments of reunion between Chaplin and his wife or his mother-in-law, joyfully identifying any hints of forgiveness, mellowing or kindliness.

The younger Chaplin's second-hand recapitulation of the story of his father's early years has occasional insights and sidelights that were evidently gleaned from conversations with Chaplin, and are nowhere else recorded. One of these is Chaplin's recollection that 'Even when I was in the orphanage, when I was roaming the streets trying to find enough to eat to keep alive, even then I thought of myself as the greatest actor in the world. I had to feel that exuberance that comes from utter confidence in yourself. Without it you go down to defeat.'

The first-hand recollections begin with the period soon after the Chaplin divorce in 1927. Young as they were, Charles recognized that he and Sydney both felt – and suffered psychologically from the fact – the absence of a loved personality. Chaplin did not contest Lita's claim for custody of the children; and for months after the divorce could not bring himself to seek his visiting rights. Indeed it was not until 1929 that he saw his sons again. The move to re-introduce the small boys to their father was made by their maternal great-grandmother, who arranged the meeting in the absence of their mother and grandmother.

After this Chaplin and his two sons remained in regular contact. Charles felt that his father was proud of them and that they also were able to fill 'some emptiness in his life'. They found him an amusing companion, always ready to entertain them with tricks or mimicry. They became conscious of his fame and popularity, and their visits to the studio instilled in them a desire to become actors themselves. Their earliest attempts in this direction were, however, firmly squashed by Chaplin himself. At the same time as Chaplin was making the second of his great international progresses, in 1931, his sons were taken by their grandmother to France, to learn the language and to broaden their education. After a year they were summoned back by their mother, since the director David Butler had expressed an interest in doing a film with the boys, who, as Chaplin's sons, had some reflected celebrity of their own. Their return to the States was the occasion for a good deal of excitement and speculation in the press; but when Chaplin heard of the career intended for them as child actors, he quickly took legal steps to prevent it. The court was sympathetic to his plea that a career would prevent his sons from enjoying a normal childhood. To his sons he explained, 'If you're really in earnest about wanting to act, going into it now would be the worst thing in the world for you, boys. You'd be typed as child actors. When you reached the gawky stage they'd drop you. Then you would have to make a complete comeback and you'd have a hard time of it, because everyone would remember you as those cute little juveniles. But if after you're grown up you still want to act, then I won't interfere.' Chaplin was no doubt remembering Jackie Coogan whose dazzling career ended abruptly with adolescence.

Soon afterwards the boys were sent to boarding school, whose tedious discipline was alleviated by weekend visits to their father's house. It was at this period, wrote Charles, that he came to see all the different aspects of his famous father: 'the strict disciplinarian, the priceless entertainer, the taciturn, moody dreamer, the wild man of Borneo with his flashes of volcanic temper. That beloved chameleon shape was to weave itself subtly through all my boyhood and was never to stop fascinating me.'

This remains perhaps the most complete and affectionate intimate portrait of Chaplin's private life. The younger Charles describes in detail the arrangements of 'house on the hill' in Hollywood, the calm and formality with which Chaplin liked his life to be ordered, his preference for old familiar furnishings (successive wives reformed that; though they were not able to make him part with a 'lucky' carpet which remained in his bedroom, worn out on the path he habitually paced when anxious or thoughtful), the three Japanese servants who anticipated his needs and – sometimes – whims.

When his father entertained, Charles noted, it was with the grace of royalty; though the entertainer was never absent for long. The son never ceased to marvel at Chaplin's gift for mimicry, whether entertaining his children with impersonations of a cat or a Sumo wrestler; or astounding guests by his imitation of Chaliapin – Chaplin explained that he couldn't sing himself, but simply imitated 'Chaliapin singing well'.

Certain of Chaplin's traits and tricks would be remembered in almost identical terms by the next generation of his children, whose spokesman, as we shall see, was his eldest son by Oona Chaplin, Michael. Both boys recalled their father's gag of going behind a sofa and appearing to walk downstairs into a supposed trap door. Both remarked upon his liking for the macabre. Charles recalls being delightedly frightened by tales of ghosts and corpses; Michael recalls a whole series of bed-time stories about the lethal doings of 'The Nice Old Man'.

Charles Chaplin Junior and his brother Sydney enjoyed happy memories of Chaplin's successive wives, Paulette Goddard and Oona O'Neill. As early teenagers they found Paulette a lively and delightful companion who found it quite natural to entertain and amuse them and take them on trips when their father was preoccupied with his work. Charles remembered his own regret when the marriage broke up, apparently without bitterness; and his father's reflection, 'It's just one of the sad things, son. That's life for you.'

As the boys grew up they were privileged observers of Chaplin at work on his features of the forties and fifties. On *Modern Times*, when they were still only children, they recalled their sympathy for Paulette Goddard, submitted to the rigorous demands he put on his artists; and his own apparent inexhaustibility, belied after hours, when he would return to the house so tired that he fell fast asleep in his car, having often not troubled to remove his costume and make-up before leaving the studio.

After *Modern Times* and a trip to the Far East with Paulette Goddard, in the course of which they were married, Chaplin struggled to find another subject suitable to her bright talents. A number of projects seem to have been begun and abandoned. He considered an oriental story, a South Seas story, and D. L. Murray's novel *Regency*. A story that was to become, twenty years later, *A Countess from Hong Kong* was designed for Goddard and Gary Cooper. An old plan for a film about Napoleon was dusted off, but then put away again. Chaplin was fascinated and repelled by Hitler, who was the same age as himself to within a few days; and who by some bizarre chance had chosen to give himself very much the same facial style as the comedian. Chaplin's horror at the activities of the Nazis in Germany was in no way mitigated by the knowledge that he was the target for some of their most vicious propaganda. The idea of a satire on Hitler was considered, worked on and then put aside for a considerable time until historical events finally determined Chaplin to embark on *The Great Dictator*. Charles Junior describes Chaplin's anxieties and then absorption with the new problems of making a dialogue film. He was less happy in the studio now: new measures of unionization had surrounded him with collaborators like make-up artists, script girls and editors whom, with his personal polytechnical skills, he had never required before.

Between *The Great Dictator* and *Monsieur Verdoux*, the Chaplin brothers had grown to manhood and seen military service. Charles recalled with touching affection their father's anxiety for their well-being and his exhortations to keep warm and not to touch anything that might be dangerous. His principal recollections of *Verdoux* were Chaplin's mixture of fascination and revulsion over the character he had created; and his relations with the comedienne Martha Raye, who plays a leading comedy role as one of the wife-murderer's victims. Miss Raye, Charles recalls, was at first over-awed at working with a comedian of such stature as Chaplin; but Chaplin so completely broke down her nervousness that she became the only collaborator in his career with the assurance to tell him it was time to break for lunch.

By the time of *Limelight* both Charles Junior and Sydney had embarked on independent careers as actors; and Chaplin gave each of them a role in the film. Sydney had the more important part, as the juvenile lead, a handsome young composer to whom the old clown, Calvero, cedes the young girl whom he has rescued from depression, breakdown and suicide. Charles had the smaller and less demanding part – little more than a walk-on – of a comic policeman in a pantomime sequence which takes place in a London music hall on the eve of the First World War.

Sydney Chaplin, Chaplin's younger son from his marriage with Lita Gray, seems only once to have set down in print his impressions of his father. The article, timed to coincide with the British premiere of *Limelight* and titled 'Father Makes a Film' was published in a long-defunct London weekly magazine, *Everybody's*; and eluded Timothy J. Lyons when he compiled his massive *Charles Chaplin: a Guide to references and resources*, with its more than fourteen hundred entries of book and periodical references to Chaplin. Though the article has something of the professional touch of a journalistic 'ghost', the impressions of the production of the film are clearly first-hand.

The article, moreover, reveals in Sydney that slightly less reverent attitude towards their father which Charles Chaplin Junior observes in his own book. Sydney recalls that it was more than four years before the making of the film that Chaplin first telephoned him to say that he had a part for him in his next picture and invited him to discuss the project – at that time still only one of several alternative films he had in mind to make. A year passed before the script had reached upwards of 700 pages and it was explained to Sydney, then eighteen stone and crew-cut, that he was to play an early-century, starving musician.

He alleges that an advertisement was placed in the professional papers saying 'Wanted: young girl to play leading lady to a comedian generally recognized as the world's greatest'; but that Arthur Laurents, who had seen Claire Bloom on the London stage in *Ring Round the Moon*, recommended her for the role which assumed such importance in the story that for the first time Chaplin shared top billing with his leading lady.

Sydney's anecdotes of Chaplin's intense industry, his concern with every aspect of the production ('if he'd had the time ... I believe that he would himself have made the shoes and sewn the skirts'), his intensive rehearsals, in which he would himself play every role, coincide with the evidence of eye-witnesses at every other Chaplin production. No-one was surprised when, after celebrating the last day of shooting, Chaplin called the unit back for three more days of retakes.

'His difficulty was to imagine how he would look in a scene which he wouldn't actually be able to see until it was filmed, and his method was to work out the moves in advance and have his stand-in go through them while he watched through the camera. One moment he'd be behind the camera, the next up 40 ft. of scaffolding explaining something to an electrician, the next strolling round the stage demonstrating some point to another actor. He did a lot of rolling around on his own account, too, for in the film he does a slapstick turn with Buster Keaton, and neither man uses doubles for these stunts.

'It was hardly surprising that father ran himself practically ragged. He was always the first to arrive at the studios in the morning and the last to leave at night. His wife Oona would come down about midday with some sandwiches and fruit pie for him. He'd go home at night quite exhausted and after dinner start right away planning the next day's work.'

Sydney recalled only one major crisis and one minor interruption. The crisis came after he had spent three days struggling to get right a very emotional scene played with Claire Bloom – a scene that lasted barely three minutes on screen. When the laboratory people reported back that they had unfortunately had a technical difficulty and destroyed the film, 'Father hit the ceiling ... but he didn't have the heart to tell Claire. He just said that he still wasn't satisfied and that he wanted to try it again.'

The minor hold-up was during the last week of shooting. 'Father was doing so much and had such a bad cold in the head that he reluctantly agreed to spend two days in bed. I hate to think what might have happened if he had not. But as soon as forty-eight hours were up, he was up too, determined to finish the film on schedule.'

Oona Chaplin, Charles Junior recalled, once joked that she would like to have a family of ten children. As it was, she settled for eight. The Chaplins had three sons and five daughters, in chronological order of arrival, Geraldine, Michael, Josephine and Victoria, all of whom were born in the United States; Eugene, Jane, Annette and Christopher, who were born after the family's emigration to Switzerland. The three eldest children made walk-on appearances in *Limelight*, as the urchins who curiously watch the drunken music-hall comic Calvero returning to his lodgings. Michael was to play a major role in *A King in New York*, as the precocious child of a left-wing couple who fall victim to the Un-American Activities witch-hunts. In a sense the role resembles that of Jackie Coogan in *The Kid*, only that the sufferings which society can inflict upon a child are, twenty years on, more subtle in their cruelty. Jackie Coogan has to face the penalties of illegitimacy and abandonment: hunger and the poorhouse. Little Rupert in *A King In New York* is hounded and brain-washed into betraying the people he loves and admires most. At its best the performance Chaplin won from his son rivalled the playing of Jackie Coogan, ranging from the comedy of Rupert's relentless political lecturing of King Shahdov to the extraordinary pathos of his final scenes.

Limelight 1952. *Chaplin with his children, Michael, Josephine and Geraldine Chaplin.*

By his own admission, Michael Chaplin was from his earliest years a natural runaway; and in any event he found it less easy than Charles Chaplin Junior to cope with the hazards of being son to a great man. To be the son of a great man, he reflected, is like living next to a huge monument; 'one spends one's life circling around it, either to remain in the shade, or to avoid its shadow'. Like his step-brother, he found that his father's creative absorption sometimes gave him little time to pay attention to the needs of a growing family of small children. 'Although my father was always a busy man, he always managed to find a moment to listen to my ideas, but he rarely had time to join me in the fulfilment of them.'

Time had not made the tasks of fatherhood any simpler. On a visit to Vevey, Charles Chaplin Junior noted that Chaplin seemed much more at ease with babies than in the days when he and his brother had been infants; but Michael Chaplin noted that 'when you're seventy-two and you believe that you've had all the experiences and are prepared to sit back and think out the rest of your life, it's maybe a little tough to try to start playing the "my boy and I are just great pals" type of father.' Youngsters of the 1960s were inclined to be impatient with the ideals of a stable and ordered family life which Chaplin had yearned for and had found with his fourth wife.

Chaplin did not approve of some of his son's friends; and the runaway habits of Michael's infancy continued, until he definitively ran away from home and settled in London. The press delighted in the misadventures of his hippy-style life, his dropping-out from R.A.D.A., and his Gretna Green marriage. When he was discovered to have drawn ten pounds from the National Assistance to help out his funds, Oona Chaplin was forced by the press into an uncharacteristically stern statement: 'He has stubbornly refused an education for three years and therefore he should get a job and go to work. If I do not wish to indulge him as a beatnik, that is my privilege – sincerely, Oona Chaplin.'

Michael Chaplin was induced to earn some more money by putting his name to a book of impressions, *I Couldn't Smoke the Grass on My Father's Lawn*. Before it was published he had second thoughts; but a legal action he brought in an attempt to stop the publication was unsuccessful. The finished text apparently was more to his liking than the original which as he said 'so horrified the judges'.

Michael Chaplin was rather less fortunate in his collaborators than his half-brother. The court case revealed that the book was the work of two 'ghosts', Charles Hamblett and Tom Merritt, whose text attributes to poor young Chaplin an awful flash hippy style which appears grotesquely antiquated two decades later.

The book was a very transparent attempt to cash in on the current news value of Michael's misadventures; and for much of its length exploits the natural spleen of a teenager rebelling against the domestic establishment. (Michael was reconciled to his father, and moved back to Switzerland before Chaplin's death.) Though from this point of view it is sad and regrettable, the book has interest both for its occasional vivid portrait glimpses and for a deep-rooted affection and admiration that unquenchably shows through all the son's ostensible resentments.

It is not hard to sympathize with the boy when he speaks of Chaplin as 'a bit of a handful as a father'. On the first page of the book he characterizes him as 'a kindly, volatile, moody, gay, self-absorbed, inventive, funny, affectionate, stern, sad, brilliant, autocratic, irrational, snobbish, splendid, silly, unjust, loving, perceptive, indifferent, sensitive, cruel, jolly, extension in-reverse of my own flesh and thought and feelings'. Michael, like the young Charles and Sydney, found the constant spotlight on the family's public life and the formality of their private life hard to cope with. Like Charles Junior, he reveals that some of the happiest times he spent in his own home were in the informality of the servants' quarters. His admiration for his father's screen work (he regretted that he did not know more of it) was unqualified; and it is clear that father and son were closest at the period when they worked together on *A King in New York*. Unfortunately, ten years old at the time, he is unable to offer very revealing recollections of Chaplin at work. He recalled crying when he heard his father reading the script over to his half-brother Sydney in Vevey; and also recalled that the only advice on acting Chaplin gave him before he embarked on the role was 'What you have to try to achieve is to be as natural as possible.'

Charles and Oona Chaplin in London in the late sixties.

Opinion of the Forties

Chaplin first had the idea for a film about Hitler in 1937. The physical similarity between the dictator and the tramp achieved by their almost identical moustaches could not be overlooked: indeed there was a popular rumour in Germany in the early thirties that Hitler had quite deliberately adopted a Chaplin moustache to cash in on a little reflected popularity. Alexander Korda seems to have been one of several people who suggested that Chaplin should return the compliment of impersonation, on the screen. Chaplin's natural indignation against such a regime as Hitler's Germany was no doubt further stimulated when Ivor Montagu sent him a copy of a repellent anti-semitic paperback published in Germany. It consisted of whole-page pictures, cunningly retouched to a point of awful ugliness, of prominent Jewish intellectuals, with accompanying text to stimulate fear and hatred of the race. Chaplin was included, with a description of him as a 'little Jewish acrobat, as disgusting as he is tedious'. The particular irony was that Chaplin was not Jewish. His 1921 book indicated positive regret to this deficiency because of his intense admiration for the qualities of the race. As early as 1916 he had quipped to a reporter who questioned him on newspaper stories about his Jewish parentage: 'I'm afraid I am not that lucky.' As time went on, however, he became more and more adamant in his refusal to contradict those who believed him to be Jewish. He told Ivor Montagu that 'anyone who denies this in respect of himself plays into the hands of the anti-Semites'. 'I did this picture for the Jews of the world', he said of *The Great Dictator*.

Chaplin plays a dual role: he is Adenoid Hynkel, the fanatical dictator of Tomania; and also a little Jewish barber (with a few physical resemblances to the old Charlie, as well as to the Führer) who is one of the country's humblest citizens. The barber is first seen as a drafted soldier at the front in the First World War. After various slapstick incidents with the instruments of war, he takes over the plane of a wounded pilot, and safely crash-lands the two of them, though he himself suffers severe amnesia as a result. He is released from hospital many years later when, as the opening title of the film explains, the world was between two World Wars – 'an interim in which Insanity cut loose, Liberty took a nosedive, and Humanity was kicked around somewhat'.

The Great Dictator *1940. Chaplin as Adenoid Hynkel.*

The Great Dictator *1940. Charlie and Hannah (Paulette Goddard) in the ghetto.*

Hynkel, leader of the Double Cross Party and given to making inflammatory speeches in the wonderfully suggestive gibberish which Chaplin invents for him, is ruler of Tomania; and in the ghetto where the little man returns to his abandoned barber shop, the Jews suffer from the persecution of Hynkel's storm troopers. It is during one of their attacks that he meets an orphan girl – played by Paulette Goddard, and bearing the name of Chaplin's own mother, Hannah. The barber is about to be strung up from a lamp-post when he is rescued by the fortuitous appearance of the pilot whose life he once saved, and who is now a party official.

121

The Great Dictator *1940. Chaplin, Paulette Goddard and Adenoid Hynkel's storm troopers.*

There are glimpses of the personal life of the dictator, planning assaults on the ghetto and the massacre of strikers and – in one of Chaplin's most justly celebrated balletic inventions – dancing with a great balloon terrestrial globe. Failing to get a desired war loan from a rich member of the Jewish community, Hynkel plans a new pogrom. When the former pilot, Schultz, opposes the plan he is arrested but escapes into the ghetto where he formulates a plot to blow up Hynkel's palace. Schultz and the barber are both arrested as members of the underground, and sent to a concentration camp. Hannah escapes to neighbouring Austerlich, unaware that Hynkel is already planning invasion.

Learning that a rival dictator Benzino Napolini of Bacteria has similar plans, Hynkel invites him to Tomania for a friendly meeting which turns into an absurd game of one-upmanship.

The barber and Schultz in the meantime have escaped from the concentration camp wearing Tomanian army uniforms. Meeting the Tomanian army on its way to invade Austerlich, the barber is mistaken for Hynkel and obliged to lead the conquering army. Hynkel, meanwhile, has been arrested whilst in mufti, by his own soldiers who take him for the barber.

The final scene disconcerted the audiences of 1940 and has continued to divide Chaplin's critics since. The barber, with Schultz at his side as his sup-

The Great Dictator *1940. Adenoid Hynkel ingratiates himself with the populace of a newly conquered country.*

posed aide, is called upon to broadcast to the world on the occasion of the invasion. At first nervous and reluctant, the barber begins his speech, 'I'm sorry, but I don't want to be an emperor. That's not my business. I don't want to rule or conquer anyone ...' The speech continues for no less than six minutes; and into it Chaplin pours all his humanist faith: '... we have lost the way. Greed has poisoned men's souls ... Machinery that gives abundance has left us in want. Our knowledge has left us cynical ...' He concludes with a direct appeal to Hannah: 'Look up, Hannah, look up!' A final close-up shows Hannah, now a captive of the Tomanian army, with the fresh wind blowing her hair and a smile on her lips, despite her tears.

Life had altered for Chaplin by the time he began production on *Monsieur Verdoux*, in 1947. The absurd, humiliating law-suits involved in the paternity charges brought by Joan Barry, as well as the growing atmosphere of political paranoia surrounding the sittings of the House Un-American Activities Committee, had suddenly toppled him from the heights of popularity that he had enjoyed for thirty years. From being the best-loved man in America he had become the most execrated. A Congressman waged a campaign to have his 'loathsome pictures' banned from exhibition; and there were all too many to support it.

The bitterness that underlies *Monsieur Verdoux* is not therefore surprising.

Chaplin's son Charles considered the film represented also that 'all the mingled fascination and horror he had felt throughout his life towards violence and the macabre.' The suggestion of a film about Landru, the celebrated French Blue-beard, was originally made to Chaplin by Orson Welles, who receives a credit on the film for the idea. Chaplin however developed the story much further to explore a notion in Von Clausewitz which had fascinated him, and which he interpreted as signifying that with murder, numbers sanctify: a general or an emperor is celebrated for killing thousands; but a small-scale operator like little Verdoux is executed as a murderer.

Verdoux, living in France in those inter-war years whose turmoils never ceased to fascinate Chaplin, is a former bank clerk who, having lost his job, has made a business out of murder, marrying and then killing rich and foolish women. Kept busy with multiple bigamy involving an assortment of victims, he also has an adored, crippled wife and a little son in the country. Seeking someone on whom to try out a new poison, he picks up a near-suicidal girl one night in the street; but having talked her into new hope, he thinks better of his plan, sends her out into the night, and instead uses the poison on a detective who has come to arrest him.

Some time later Verdoux and the girl meet again, Verdoux has been ruined in the stock market crash and has lost his wife and child. The girl is now married to a rich munitions manufacturer; Verdoux wryly reflects that that is the business he should have been in: it is sure to pay dividends soon. At that moment he is recognized by the family of one of his victims; and calmly submits to arrest.

In court, the gentle Verdoux is pilloried as a 'cruel and cynical monster'. Asked if he has anything to say, he asks, 'Mass killing – does not the world encourage it? I'm an amateur in comparison.'

It was, however, the final sequence of the film, the visit of a priest to Verdoux in the death cell, which principally aroused the anxiety of the Breen Office – the American censorship authority of those years – and the ire of Chaplin's more bigoted critics. Verdoux debates amiably with the priest, and to his concluding, 'May God have mercy on your soul' replies cheerfully, 'Why not? After all it belongs to him.'

*   *   *

The contemporary press for *The Great Dictator* was in general enthusiastic. Had people known as much at that stage of the war about Hitler's camps and gas chambers and genocidal policies as they were later to know, commentators might of course have been more uneasy about the whole enterprise.

The première audience was surprised and a little disconcerted by the length and the uncompromised, passionate seriousness of the final speech. Many, however, felt with Basil Wright, the distinguished British film maker and critic, that what the speech lacked in literary distinction was compensated by the sincerity of Chaplin's delivery. 'The speech,' wrote the scholarly Paul

Monsieur Verdoux *1946. Monsieur and Madame Verdoux at home (Chaplin and Mady Correll).*

Goodman in *The Partisan Review*, 'is too long, it is not even well spoken throughout, but when he says, "We think too much and feel too little" and "Now we must fight!" – we know that the context for the truth or falsity of these propositions has been fairly given to us by the speaker. If this isn't meant from the heart, we have been deceived for twenty-five years.'

Goodman's review of the film remains one of the most interesting single essays in criticism of Chaplin's cinema. It has the merit of combining a close critical analysis with an open-hearted emotional response. He frankly acknowledges lack of comic continuity, poor timing, 'calamitous music', lapses in style; but counters, 'what possibly is the meaning of 'lapses in style' when applied to Charlie Chaplin. The film is something different and something better than the 'grandiose failure' that some critics found it.'

Monsieur Verdoux *1946*.

However Goodman perceives a profound difference between this Chaplin film and what had gone before, in the films made between 1914 and 1935. 'The Little Man,' he argues, 'was always isolated in his inability to adjust to society; but that society was in principle *approved*, so that the pathetic humour lay in the hero's well-intentioned efforts to make an adjustment to society.' In *The Great Dictator*, however, the environment is not in principle approved, so that 'the poet finds suddenly that it is wicked to try to make an adjustment to the Nazi order. The result of this is that a completely different kind of comedy appears, involving comic invective and directive satire. At the same time the "natural" society represented by the ghetto, as contrast to the "unnatural" environment of the dictator's creation, which is the object of satire, becomes a non-comic object of desire.' Thus, in Goodman's analysis, there are three distinct kinds of comedy in the film: (a) Invective against the unnatural Nazi regime; (b) sentimental handling of the 'natural' life of the ghetto; and (c) slapstick in the two environments.

The invective against Hynkel-Hitler is 'to my taste all-powerful, disgust expressed by the basest tricks of low vaudeville, gibberish, belching, dirty words, and radio static. You will not find the like outside of Juvenal.' The

The Great Dictator *1940. The Jewish barber in the hands of Hynkel's storm troopers.*

The Great Dictator *1940. The Jewish barber has been mistaken for the Great Dictator. On the right, Reginald Gardiner.*

sentimental element, on the other hand, Goodman finds 'catastrophic'; and yet – because of its creator's own wholly non-ironic belief in it, 'paradoxically, I shall almost argue that it is just these horrors which lead to a kind of triumph, the major triumph, of the film as a whole'. The slapstick and burlesque weaken the force of the invective, because 'Chaplin slapstick almost always turns out with the victim made amiable'. The elements are variable; but 'except for a few documentaries, like Joris Ivens' *Spanish Earth, The Great Dictator* strikes me – obviously I cannot speak for any one else on this point – as the only earnest propaganda film.'

The opinion of another academic, Rudolf Arnheim, is especially interesting, since Arnheim was a German Jew who had been forced to flee from Hitler to the United States. Only two artists, Arnheim suggested, could have made a great film on Hitler – Erich von Stroheim and Chaplin. Chaplin recognized the great theme of the day and actually attempted it, despite the risks – artistic as well as personal. *The Great Dictator,* he found, was a film full of the authentic Chaplin genius, far above anything the pleasure industry was capable of producing – and yet 'there are many of us who feel that in it Chaplin did not fully realize his intention'.

Chaplin, he continued, had seemed the David who could meet this Goliath with weapons of the spirit, with ridicule. Chaplin's great creation, Charlie, represents the inadequacies, the uncertainties and the aspirations of that lower middle class from which Hitler sprang. Apart from the physical similarity, Chaplin played the Führer to perfection – 'this is a pure, an illuminating piece of art'. Yet what the portrait shows is simply a ridiculous, mad and cruel man whose elimination might restore peace and order to the world. This he contended, though it represented a view widely held at the time, was not a true picture of the situation. The fight was not against a man but against a whole system.

The system, he felt would have given itself admirably to satire: 'there is much more Chaplin in fascist reality than in *The Great Dictator*'. The falsity of its propaganda, the hollowness of its boasting and the coexistence of enormously contrasting social elements he felt were ideal subjects for satire: 'Is there any better subject for satire than the false front?' But, he felt, Chaplin had failed to use satire in his treatment of the Nazi system. He had tried to use pity instead of understanding. But his depictions of the pogroms, of the beatings in the ghetto, perforce fell very short of the reality of the Nazi horror. Likewise the portraits of the dictators and their creatures fell short of satire, turning them into buffoons. The sign of Chaplin's failure in his main purpose was the need, in the final scene to 'say directly what he had failed to convey artistically'.

Arnheim clearly felt that Chaplin had achieved far, far more than the 'serious' anti-Nazi films of the day, the melodramas of horror, violence and cruelty that had become a new kind of gangster film. But he had not achieved all that a Chaplin might have done:

'Charles Chaplin is the only artist who holds the secret weapon of mortal laughter. Not the laughter of superficial gibing that self-complacently underrates the enemy and ignores the danger, but rather the profound laughter of the sage who despises physical violence, even the threat of death, because behind it he has discovered the spiritual weakness, stupidity, and falseness of his antagonist. Chaplin could have opened the eyes of a world enchanted by the spell of force and material success. But instead of unmasking the common enemy, fascism, Chaplin unmasked a single man, "The Great Dictator". And that is why I feel that this good film should have been better.' (Arnheim's review appeared in the Winter 1940 issue of *Films*.)

In the six and a half years that elapsed between the release of *The Great Dictator* and *Monsieur Verdoux* Chaplin's troubles over the Joan Barry paternity case and the growth of the McCarthyist spirit had served to effect a reversal in the public's estimation such as few artists since Oscar Wilde had experienced. Even the most critical of writers sincerely wanted to like *The Great Dictator*. A very large part of those who wrote about *Monsieur Verdoux* in the United States felt a positive duty and determination to execrate *any* work by this artist. Beside the hysterical anger which infused many notices in the more popular press, Howard Barnes in the *Herald Tribune* appeared quite mild: 'It has little entertainment weight, either as somber symbolism or sheer nonsense ... It is also something of an affront to the intelligence.'

Ironically and happily, while the invective and abuse is mostly forgotten, the writings of one outstanding champion of the film are still remembered.

James Agee, who was to die of a heart attack at the age of 45, in 1955, remains one of the finest writers who applied their talents to film criticism. He wrote gracefully and wittily; he had the ability to be very funny without ever scoring off a film that did not deserve it; he brought to his job great knowledge, a fine intelligence, and (he made you feel) a conscience and a soul. Towards the end of his life he wrote some screenplays, among them *The African Queen* and *Night of the Hunter*. His critical work mostly appeared in periodicals; he was film critic of *Time* from 1941 to 1948, and for *The Nation* from 1942 to 1948. Thus he was able to review *Monsieur Verdoux* in two places and for two audiences. Ahead of his *Nation* review, on 10th May 1947 he issued his readers with due warning: 'let me say that I think it is one of the best movies ever made, easily the most exciting and most beautiful since *Modern Times*. I will add that I think most of the press on the picture, and on Chaplin, is beyond disgrace.'

To confirm his view, he headed his article of 31st May 1947, '*Monsieur Verdoux* – I'; and then went on to do two sequent articles, on 14th June and 21st June, appropriately numbered 'II' and 'III'. He began the first of his articles with the modest wish that 'these notes may faintly suggest the frame-by-frame appreciation, the gratitude, and the tribute which we owe this great poet and his great poem'. He urged his readers to disregard practically everything they might have read about the film. It was of interest, he said, chiefly as the measure of the difference between 'the thing a man of genius puts before the world' and 'the things the world is equipped to see in it'. Though he felt there was neither room nor reason to analyse or argue with most of these opinions, he nevertheless dealt with specific charges repeatedly made against the film.

To the charge that the film was *not funny*, Agee countered that not much of it was, unless the spectator had an eye and mind for the cold nihilistic irony which Chaplin employed. He gave even shorter shrift to those who objected on the score of morals; on grounds of bad taste; because Chaplin had abandoned his tramp character; because he allowed Martha Raye to steal her scenes from him; or because other roles were miscast.

To criticism of the writing, Agee countered that verbally the film was inferior to its visual achievements, which is merely to say that it was one of the most talented screenplays ever written. To those who tried to fault the direction, he compared the film to *Modern Times* and Dovzhenko's *Frontier* – 'there has been none (as brilliant) since'. The production had been criticized as stingy and unlike France in the settings. Agee on the contrary saw it as a manifesto against the prevailing vulgarity of opulence that tainted Hollywood. 'Verdoux's France is a highly intelligent paraphrase'. Equally Agee dismissed charges that Chaplin's methods were antiquated; in particular he

Monsieur Verdoux *1946. Chaplin with Martha Raye, as a tricky victim.*

pointed out what very many later writers have failed to recognize that when Chaplin revives some ancient cliché, like the train wheels which punctuate and commentate the action of *Verdoux*, it is with wit, irony and a sense of parody – but at the same time an appreciation of the proper dramatic value of any device, however well-worn it may be.

Agee ended his first article with the words, 'to be continued'. In the second section of his serial review, Agee, having spent what might seem an inordinate space on regretting lack of space to praise Chaplin's acting, the richness and quality of the film, and its fun, devotes himself to a close analysis of Verdoux's character and its meaning. Clearly, he said, it chimed with a degree of disillusion and misanthropy in the man himself: 'it is ... fascinating as a study of the relationship between ends and means, a metaphor for the modern personality – that is, a typical "responsible" personality reacting to contemporary pressures according to the logic of contemporary ethics ...'

131

Monsieur Verdoux *1946. Chaplin and Barbara Slater.*

'... He has made the assumption that most people make, today – one of the chief assumptions on which modern civilization rests. That is, that in order to preserve intact in such a world as this those aspects of the personality which are best and dearest to one, it is necessary to exercise all that is worst in one; and that it is impossible to do this effectively if one communicates honestly with one's best. Accordingly the personality which, until the world struck that living down, lived in poverty and docility, but happily, is broken and segregated.'

By 21st January 1947, when the third part of Agee's review appeared, it was necessary to inform his readers that the film had been withdrawn by United Artists, who planned to reissue it with a new advertising campaign. The consolation for Agee was that it was 'permanent, if any work done during the past twenty years is permanent'. In the third chapter of his review he concentrates on the complexity of the moral issues Chaplin's story raises. Chaplin, he concluded, had set aside his tramp character, 'to give his century its truest portrait of the upright citizen'.

It is curious to turn back from this three-part eulogium, to Agee's review in *Time*, which appeared almost four weeks before the first of the *Nation* articles. The *Time* piece is enthusiastic ('one of the most notable pictures in years') but by no means so unqualified in its praise. '*Monsieur Verdoux* has serious shortcomings, both as popular entertainment and as a work of art.' 'It has its blurs and failures. Finely cut and paced as it is, the picture goes on so long, and under such darkness and chill, that the lazier-minded type of cinemagoers will probably get tired. Chaplin overexerts, and apparently overestimates, a writing talent which, though vigorous and unconventional, weighs light beside his acting gifts.'

What had happened in between the two reviews was not really a change of mind. Agee's generous and emotional being had simply reacted to the brutality with which the press and the public had set out to pillory Chaplin.

After *Verdoux*, Agee never missed an opportunity to praise the name of Chaplin, at a time when that name was anathema to so many Americans. At Christmas 1947, he wrote a scathing article on the Hollywood activities at the House Un-American Activities Committee and on the Catholic Veterans' holy war against Chaplin. 'I believe', he said, 'that a democracy which cannot contain all its enemies, of whatever kind or virulence, is finished as a democracy.' 'It seems to me that the mere conception of a vigorous and genuine democracy, to say nothing embarrassing about its successful practice, depends on a capacity for faith in human beings so strong that on its basis one can dare to assume that goodness and intelligence will generally prevail over stupidity and evil.' Had he written nothing else but that article, at that time, Agee would still have been remembered as a rare spirit.

The best remembered and most often quoted of all James Agee's writings however remains the cover story he contributed to *Life* magazine on 3rd September 1949, entitled *Comedy's Greatest Era*. The article is said to have received one of the most enthusiastic responses recalled in the history of the magazine. It came at a time when the silent comedians of whom Agee wrote so vividly were all but forgotten; and the impact of the article did very much to restore the reputations of artists like Keaton, Harry Langdon, Harold Lloyd, Fatty Arbuckle, and their contemporaries. Inevitably the central section of the article deals with the art of Chaplin; and included Agee's ultimate tribute: 'The finest pantomine, the deepest emotion, the richest and most poignant poetry were in Chaplin's work.'

*　　*　　*

An 'unauthorized biography' by Gerith von Ulm, *Charlie Chaplin: King of Tragedy* had appeared in 1940; and after this the industry of Chaplin books got really under way. In 1945 Theodore Huff's *Index to the Creative Work of Charles Spencer Chaplin* was published by the British Film Institute, to provide the first reliable record of Chaplin's work and collaborators. In 1948 the poet and critic Parker Tyler published *Chaplin Last of the Clowns*; and like Agee's articles, the great significance of the book was its appearance at this moment when Chaplin's popularity was lowest. The layout and typography of the book reflect the strongly 'period' quality of its content. Leaning heavily upon both the fact and the speculative fancy of Miss Von Ulm's biography of eight years earlier, Tyler weaves a Freudian and symbolist interpretation of Chaplin as man and Charlie as creation. For instance, 'if we look for the epos, or essentially biographic pattern, in the comic history of Charlie, the tramp hero, we find side by side an economic and aesthetic reality; the clown is a professional, a highly successful artist in comedy miming, and a lover whose life is symbolically reflected by the basically creative epos of his art', etc. Tyler's, though, was a work of love; and that mattered at this moment in Chaplin's career.

Monsieur Verdoux *1946*.

In exile: Charles and Oona Chaplin in Switzerland. Behind them, Josephine Chaplin, their daughter, and a friend.

The Fall

The nineteen-forties were perhaps the darkest era in American history. The United States entered the second World War in 1941; and the decade ended with the Communist witch-hunts which saw some of the most vicious political persecution ever experienced in a Western democracy, and did grievous injury to the national morale. For Chaplin personally these were the most bitter years he had experienced. One of the best-loved men in the entire world at the start of the decade, he found himself by the end of it execrated by a vocal section of American opinon. In 1952 he sought permanent exile from the country he had made his home, and to which he had brought so much lustre, during thirty-eight years.

The exile began without Chaplin's own premeditation. On Wednesday 17th September 1952, with his wife Oona and their four children, he set sail from New York on the *Queen Elizabeth* to attend the London première of *Limelight*. The liner had only been at sea forty-eight hours when the American Attorney-General, James McGranery, announced in Washington that he had ordered an inquiry to determine whether Chaplin should be allowed back into the United States. He had, he said, instructed the immigration authorities to hold Chaplin 'if and when he returns' until an official hearing could decide whether he was admissible under American law.

Only on September 30th did the Justice Department make specific their charges against the comedian. The Attorney-General stated: 'He has been publicly charged with being a member of the Communist Party, and with grave moral charges, and with making statements that would indicate a leering, sneering attitude towards a country whose hospitality has enriched him.' The charges were astounding; but not unusual in those years of public paranoia.

Chaplin had always been a natural target for successive generations of moralists who gained self esteem and vicarious excitement from attacking the standards of the film colony. Chaplin had been married four times, and the first two of these marriages had ended in noisy divorce actions. His fourth marriage, to the eighteen-year-old daughter of Eugene O'Neill, when he was already fifty-four excited further indignation. It did not help that he was a foreigner, who had never sought American citizenship.

Chaplin was successful, rich, attractive to women and, for long periods between marriages, in a state of bachelorhood. He never made a secret of his admiration for beautiful women, which made him distinctly vulnerable to the opportunists among them. In his bachelor years of the early nineteen-forties, Joan Barry had entered his life.

Barry, whom Chaplin described as 'a big handsome woman of twenty-two' and who was involved in a long affair with another rich man, the oil magnate J. Paul Getty, was introduced to Chaplin at her own request by his friend Tim Durant. After the first meeting she pursued Chaplin so insistently as to rouse his suspicions; but 'Persistence is the road to accomplishment. Thus she achieved her object and I began to see her often.' Having met in May 1941 their friendship evidently continued for around a year. Sometime in the early autumn of 1942 Chaplin decided that the girl might have some acting talent, considered her for the role in his projected production of Paul Vincent Carroll's *Shadow and Substance*, put her under contract to the Chaplin Studio at a salary of seventy-five dollars a week, and enrolled her in Max Reinhardt's school of acting. Meanwhile however Barry's behaviour had become obstreperous and erratic, and when she announced that she had given up attendance at the Reinhardt school and didn't want to be an actress, he rather happily agreed to her offer to cancel the contract in consideration of five thousand dollars and her own and her mother's fares back to New York.

Still he was not rid of her. When he arrived in New York to speak at a public meeting in support of a second front in Europe, Barry insisted on seeing him – though Chaplin insisted that the meeting took place in the presence, for the whole time, of Tim Durant. Subsequently she reappeared in Hollywood, resumed her practice of turning up at the Chaplin house to cause scandals. She announced that she was six months' pregnant (which, said Chaplin, 'was certainly no concern of mine'); and contrived to force Chaplin to call the police and have her arrested on his premises.

'A few hours later the newspapers were black with headlines. I was pilloried, excoriated and vilified: Chaplin, the father of her unborn child, had had her arrested, had left her destitute.'

A week later Joan Barry brought a paternity suit against Chaplin. Their lawyers agreed, however, that if Chaplin paid Miss Barry a sum in the region of sixteen thousand dollars to cover maintenance of herself and the child and lawyers' fees, she would permit the infant to undergo a series of blood tests and thereafter drop the suit if the tests proved conclusively that Chaplin was not the child's father.

Meanwhile however the Federal authorities seized the opportunity to indict Chaplin under the so-called Mann Act, a measure passed by Congress in 1919 to combat commercial prostitution and which in subsequent years had been regularly abused by ingenious and unscrupulous lawyers; as Chaplin reflected, 'Should a man accompany his divorced wife over the border to another state, and should he have intercourse with her, he has committed an offence against the Mann Act.'

The indictment claimed that on 5th October 1942 – the date when Chaplin had given Mrs and Miss Barry their fares to New York – he had 'feloniously transported and caused to be transported Joan Barry from Los Angeles to the city of New York' for immoral purposes.

The State case depended on establishing that Chaplin had had sexual relations with Miss Barry on the occasion of his visit to New York for the Second Front speech. The defence contention was that because of her insistence Chaplin did meet the girl on this occasion, but only for half an hour and then all the time in the presence of Tim Durant. Chaplin's counsel Jerry Giesler ridiculed the Prosecution contention that Chaplin should transport Barry 4,000 miles for the purpose of a single intimacy when the girl 'would have given her body to him at any time or place'. The Prosecution rather feebly countered, 'Do you think it's any pleasure for a young girl to get up on the witness stand and tell an incident of this kind?'

The Jury of seven women and five men deliberated for several hours during which Chaplin waited in growing anxiety: a guilty verdict could have meant twenty-three years' imprisonment and a fine of $26,000 and possible deportation. In a first ballot five jurors were for guilty, six for not guilty, with one abstention. Not until the fourth ballot was a unanimous vote of 'not guilty' reached. Chaplin thanked each juror; and as he shook hands with Mrs Edythe Lewis, the wife of a canned goods broker, she told him, 'It's all right, Charlie. It's still a free country ... I could see you from the window of the jury room pacing up and down, and I so wanted to tell you not to worry. But for two persons we could have come to a decision in ten minutes.'

The trial ended on 4th April 1944. Barry's child had been born on 3rd October 1943; and in February 1944 the blood tests on the baby, Carol Ann, were performed by physicians representing the two parties, with a third as an independent observer. The tests showed conclusively that Chaplin could not be father of the child; and Chaplin's lawyers moved for the dismissal of the paternity suit, as agreed in advance.

But neither the law nor Miss Barry had done with Chaplin. The Judge of the Superior Court overruled the motion for a dismissal; while the Court of Los Angeles assumed guardianship of Carol Ann. In consequence it was the Court, and not the child's previous guardian Mrs Gertrude Barry, who was suing Chaplin when the paternity trial began in December 1944.

In the witness box Joan Barry testified that the conception took place in December 1942, and offered a circumstantial description of the events which commenced with her entering the Chaplin home and threatening the comedian with a pistol. Chaplin agreed with this part of the story but strenuously denied that any intimacy took place. The defence testimony depended on proving that Barry at this time was having an affair with 'an oil man' (which she denied) and on the blood tests which established the impossibility of Chaplin being the father of Carol Ann.

The Prosecution Attorney, Joseph Scott, was a grey-haired, bushy-browed and craggy-faced lawyer of the old histrionic school who bludgeoned the jury with emotional appeals, and subjected the defendant to a kind of abuse that, forty years on, seems hardly believable: 'a little runt of a Svengali' was one of the milder insults he applied. This 'wretched specimen of a man', he said, 'should be made to realize the law treats him the same as a man down on Skid Row'. The abuse seemed crude; but comments like these were well calculated to make emotive use of innate resentments of the defendant's fame and wealth.

When the jury voted seven to five for Chaplin's acquittal, the judge declared a mistrial, and ordered a new trial, which began on 12th August 1944. This time the Jury was more amenable to emotion – not necessarily because it numbered eleven women and one man. When an eleven to one decision against Chaplin was agreed, the dissenter was a woman, who said 'I'm not upholding Mr Chaplin at all ... only I don't think he was the father of the child.'

Nine years later the California court would have agreed with her: in 1953 it finally fell into line with most other legislatures, with a ruling that prohibited any further litigation against a defendant whom blood tests have proved cannot be the father of the child. But this was too late to save Chaplin falling victim to misplaced hostile sentiment, or to suffer smears that were to prove indelible for many years. As Attorney-General McGranery's charges showed, the grotesque Barry affair was to weigh heavily against him when he found himself one of the victims of the political persecution of the later nineteen-forties.

In Chaplin's 1921 record of *My Trip Abroad* there is a curious foreboding of the troubles that were to hit him almost forty years later. He reports his grilling by reporters as he is leaving the United States; and with some extra-ordinary prescient irony refers to one of them as 'another district attorney:

'Another district attorney took the floor.

'"Mr Chaplin, are you a Bolshevik?"

'"No."

'"Then why are you going to Europe?"

'"For a holiday."

'"What holiday?"'

The style of questioning is eerily familiar from the Alice-in-Wonderland quizzes of the House Committee on Un-American activities.

The troubles began in earnest with the making of *Monsieur Verdoux*. Orson Welles had given the comedian the idea of building a film out of the story of Landru, the notorious multiple murderer. Out of this Chaplin developed the notion of Verdoux, a gentle little French bourgeois, struggling to maintain his sick wife and family in France in the 1920s, and eventually surviving by making a well-organized business out of marrying and murdering rich widows.

When the script was first submitted to the censorship – the Breen Office – it was rejected out of hand on account of its totally unacceptable morality;

but later Chaplin managed to persuade them to accept it, with some emendations. The Breen Office made it clear that their principal objections lay in the parallels which Verdoux draws between his own approach to murder as a private enterprise business, and the authorized operation of murder as a business by the state, in the form of war; and to the final scene, in which Verdoux rather rationally and confidently discusses morality with the priest who visits him in the condemned cell, with aphoristic comments like 'I am at peace with God. My conflict is with man.' Chaplin remarked that when he showed the finished film to the Legion of Decency, most of the representatives looked 'glum'.

While Chaplin was still filming *Monsieur Verdoux*, which was eventually released in April 1947, the House Committee on Un-American Activities had begun its work. Chaplin was one of the earliest to be called. He first heard of the summons through the newspapers, and promptly fired off a telegram to Representative J. Parnell Thomas, Chairman of the House Committee, couched in terms of deep sarcasm. 'I notice from your publicity,' Chaplin began, 'that I am to be quizzed by the House Un-American Activities Committee in Washington in September ... Forgive me for this premature acceptance of your headlines newspaper invitation ...' He went on to suggest that the Chairman could find more convenient, less public and certainly less expensive ways of discovering whether or not he was a Communist; and concluded, 'While you are preparing your engraved sub-poena I will give you a hint on where I stand. I am not a Communist. I am a peacemonger.'

The telegram was reprinted in the national press. Chaplin was subpoenaed to testify in due course, but the appearance was three times postponed; and finally Chaplin received a 'surprisingly courteous reply to the effect that my appearance would not be necessary, and that I could consider the matter closed'.

Chaplin's detractors were not to be deterred merely because the Committee cried off. In that Cold War era reactionary pressure groups like the American Legion and the Catholic War Veterans discovered they could wield considerable power on public opinion, and effect devastating commercial boycotts by their propaganda and picketing.

The first volleys were fired at the press conference for the New York première of *Monsieur Verdoux*. The conference was held in the Grand Ballroom of the Gotham Hotel at 55th Street. The room was crowded; representatives had turned up from every major paper in the United States, clearly scenting some kind of trouble. Chaplin started the conference off with a humorous exhortation to 'Proceed with the butchery'. He can hardly have been aware how appropriate was this choice of words.

It was clear from the start that a number of hostile questioners had managed to get into the conference, the most vocal of them being one James W. Fay who claimed to represent the publication *Catholic War Veterans*. Subsequently Fay was to become President of the Guild of Catholic Lawyers in New York, and National Commander of the 200,000-strong veterans' group. The questioning started with some mild sniping about the credit due to Orson Welles for the story of *Monsieur Verdoux*, and whether Chaplin was not involved in some combine with the Soviet Union to assure the film's exhibition there. Then someone attacked directly with 'There have been several stories in the press accusing you more or less of being a fellow-traveller, a Communist sympathizer. Could you define your present political beliefs, sir?' Chaplin parried the question, along with others asking, if he was not a Communist was he a sympathizer? but fell into a new trap: 'I have never belonged to any political party in my life, and I have never voted in my life.' At this point Fay launched in with questions, or rather charges, relating to Chaplin's failure of responsibility and respect to the country of his residence. When Chaplin countered with statements about the large sums in tax he contributed to the United States, Fay introduced a somewhat mystifying issue about veterans also paying their taxes.

'The problem is,' Chaplin began; 'What is it that you are objecting to?'

'I'm objecting,' pursued the odious Fay, 'to your particular stand that you have no patriotic feelings about this country or any other country.'

'I think you're . . .' Chaplin began; but Fay thundered on: 'You've worked here, you've made your money here, you went around in the last war when you should have been serving Great Britain, you were here selling bonds, so it stated in the papers that I read, and I think that you as a citizen here – or rather a resident here – taking our money should have done more.'

Chaplin defended himself gallantly: 'Well that's another question of opinion,' he began after a slight pause (the whole conference, even the more hostile sections, seem to have been stunned by Fay's intemperate outburst). 'I say I think it's rather dictatorial on your part to say as how I should apply my patriotism. I have patriotism and I had patriotism in this way and I showed it and I did a great deal for the war effort but it was never advertised here. Now, whether you say that you object to me for not having patriotism is a qualified thing. I've been that way ever since I have been a young child. I cannot help it. I've travelled all over the world and my patriotism doesn't rest with one class. It rests with the whole world – the pity of the whole world and the common people, and that includes even those who object to my – that sort of patriotism.'

Fay appears to have been for the moment silenced; but other questioners led the discussion into channels which were equally treacherous. He was asked if he had intended to create sympathy for Verdoux, a murderer. 'No,' he answered; 'I wanted to create a pity for all humanity under certain drastic circumstances.' He was asked about his wartime activities; and explained how his by now notorious 'Second Front' speech came about because he substituted for Ambassador Davies who was ill and unable to make a speech as planned in San Francisco; and that he 'spoke what was in my heart, what was in my mind'.

Next he was challenged on his friendship with Hanns Eisler. Yes, said Chaplin, he was a personal friend, and 'I am very proud of the fact'. Did he think Eisler was a Communist? 'I know he is a fine artist and a great musician and a very sympathetic friend.' Would it make any difference if he were a Communist? 'No it wouldn't.' Or a Soviet agent? Even Chaplin could hardly cope with that line of non-sequitur.

The hostile questioners attempted to lead him into political discussion, asking him if he could deny that Russian propaganda techniques and Russian expansion were not similar in style to the Nazi techniques he had decried; whether his argument was that modern civilization was making mass murderers of us all ('All my life I have always loathed and abhorred violence'); what he would do with the atomic bomb ('I'm not a politician'); why he had never taken American citizenship ('I'm not nationalistic').

There was a pause in the inquisition while a more friendly questioner told Chaplin that he believed – and 'it seems to me that I am in the minority here' – that he should have the right to think what he wished, though he believed Chaplin had 'stopped being such a good comedian since your pictures have been bringing messages – so-called'. Chaplin replied that it was his privilege to think so; and the man pursued, 'Are you going to make any more pictures for children – that children like?' Chaplin rather sharply replied that he would make the pictures that he liked, 'because if I like something – I'm pretty commonplace – then children ought to like it'. This set off the baying hounds again: 'Would you – you have children – would you let *them* see your picture?'

Most of the ammunition seemed now spent, however; and the questioning went on to the more ordinary business of press conferences – was there special significance to making a film about the Depression period; how closely was Verdoux modelled on Landru, was he going to make more pictures with the tramp, or more pictures with a message?

There was one final attempt to rekindle the hostility 'Mr Chaplin, have you ever used the proceeds of your films overseas, abroad, for resistance work and for the alleviation of poverty and for – well, the alleviation of poverty of the people abroad. For example, in France – were the proceeds of *The Great Dictator* used for the salvation of people in D. P. camps, political refugees ...' The question was pursued, despite Chaplin's evident bewilderment as to where it was supposed to lead until a tactful spokesman for United Artists brought the questioning to an end.

The single touching aspect of the whole unseemly event had come towards the end of the questioning when James Agee, the critic of *The Nation*, had stood up in the gallery, so angry that his voice trembled and his words were so confused that Chaplin had to ask him to repeat his statement. As far as it could be heard (and like the rest of the quotations in the foregoing account it is taken from a recording made on the spot by George Wallach and reprinted in transcript in *Film Comment* in 1969), Agee's protest ran:

'What are people who care a damn about freedom – who really care for it – think of a country and the people in it, who congratulate themselves upon this country as the finest on earth and as a "free country", when so many of the people in this country pry into what a man's citizenship is, try to tell him his business from hour to hour and from day to day and exert a public moral blackmail against him for not becoming an American citizen – for his political views and for not entertaining troops in the manner – in the way they think he should. What is to be thought of a general country where those people are thought well of?'

The demonstration at the *Verdoux* press conference, however, was only the first volley of the campaign that was now to be waged without respite against Chaplin. In December 1947 the Catholic War Veterans of New York sent a telegram urging the Attorney General and Secretary of State to investigate 'the activities of Charles Chaplin'.

These activities, it was alleged involved attempts to prevent the deportation of Hanns Eisler (an attempt, it was said, 'to interfere with the activities of a duly elected representative of our citizens'). Chaplin, it was revealed with suitable horror, had allegedly sent a message to the Communist Pablo Picasso, asking him to protest against the deportation. A Republican Senator declared that it all 'skirts perilously close to treason'.

In such an atmosphere of hysterical malevolence towards Chaplin, Attorney General McGranery's announcement, when Chaplin was on the high seas *en route* to the European premières of *Limelight*, surprised fewer people than in more temperate times it might have done. Many exulted. Chaplin had no right, wrote the widely syndicated and dedicatedly Republican Hedda Hopper, 'to go against our customs, to abhor everything we stand for, to throw our hospitality back in our faces ... I abhor what he stands for ... Good riddance to bad rubbish.'

The American Legion were inspired to picket Chaplin's new film, *Limelight*, with such success that the Legion's Commander was able to announce proudly that theatres were withdrawing the film pending the outcome of the investigation of Chaplin by the Justice Department.

Chaplin himself remained silent for a while; as a later chapter discusses, he was concerned not to aggravate his position, and thereby risk losing all his economic assets in the United States, by giving any impression that he had no intention of returning to answer the Attorney General. Finally however, with his affairs safely cleared up, in April 1953 he turned in his re-entry permit with the statement: 'It is not easy to uproot myself and my family from a country where I have lived for forty years, without a feeling of sadness.

'But since the end of the last World War I have been the object of lies and vicious propaganda by powerful reactionary groups who by their influence and the aid of America's yellow press have created an unhealthy atmosphere in which liberal-minded individuals can be singled out and persecuted. Under these conditions I find it virtually impossible to continue my motion picture work and I have therefore given up my residence in the United States.'

Self-Portrait III: The Exile

Self-Portrait: III

The final chapters of Chaplin's 1964 Autobiography describe, with all the feeling his writing, whatever its idiosyncracies, was singularly equipped to convey, the sensations and the eventual serenity of an exile. The last Atlantic sea trip was made on the *Queen Elizabeth*. Chaplin, quite unable, it seemed, to escape trouble, had to steal aboard the ship and remain hidden to avoid process-servers attempting to deliver a summons relating to a suit against United Artists by a former employee. This resulted in a sad little incident. The loyal James Agee had come to the dock to see them off; and Oona Chaplin had told him that Chaplin would wave to him from the porthole. Chaplin waved his Fedora wildly, and Agee searched the boat; but 'Jim never did see me; and that was the last I ever saw of Jim, standing alone as though apart from the world, peering and searching. Two years later he died of a heart attack'.

The ship was two days out when Chaplin received the radio cable telling him he was barred from the United States until he had answered an Immigration Board of Enquiry on charges of political offences and moral turpitude. Chaplin was instantly besieged by the press, demanding statements. He recalled that he would have liked to have told them that 'the sooner I was rid of that hate-beleagured atmosphere the better, that I was fed up with America's insults and moral pomposity'. But he was obliged to consider that everything he possessed was in the United States, and he could not risk the Government thinking up some means to confiscate it. He recognized that he could now expect 'any unscrupulous action from them'. He therefore retaliated with what he described as 'a pompous statement' to the effect that he would return to answer the charges, and that the re-entry permit that was now denied had been given him in good faith by the United States Government.

In Europe, at least, he found sympathy. A press conference at Cherbourg was exhausting, but the press-men were on his side. At Waterloo, the Chaplins were met by the usual crowd – not the terrifying, adoring multitudes of 1921, but enough to show that London still honoured Chaplin as a son.

This was the first time Chaplin had been accompanied by a wife and family to whom he could show off his native city and country; and he touchingly relates his concern that both should come up to their expectations and confirm his own nostalgic memories. Illustrative of his gift for the vivid, evocative phrase is his comment on the new Waterloo Bridge, which the family could see from their suite in the Savoy: 'although beautiful, it meant little to me now, only that its road led over to my boyhood'.

In the twenty years since his last visit to London in 1931 much of the skyline had been altered by the war and modern building. 'Half of my boyhood had gone in the charred embers of its sooty, vacant lots.' He was never to tire, however, of showing Oona and his growing family the places he remembered – the houses in Kennington where the Chaplin family had lodged when Charles and Sydney were boys (he was sad to see 3 Pownall Terrace, his home for some years, awaiting demolition) and the elegant squares of Belgravia, which he remembered in days when they were grand private houses, but which had now descended the social scale to office use.

Oona Chaplin flew back to California to begin the business involved in extricating their property from the United States – a separation that made Chaplin understandably anxious. On her return she was able to report that in their absence FBI men had called twice at their home, bullying the domestic

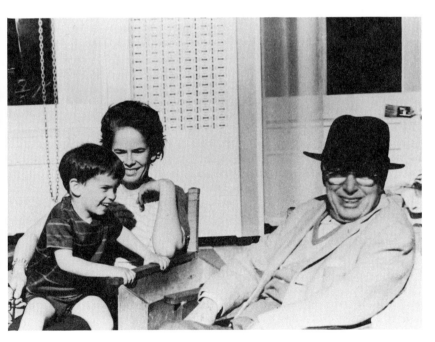

At Vevey, Charles and Oona Chaplin with one of their sons.

staff who still remained, because they were unable to provide evidence of scandalous occurrences in the Chaplin home.

At this point in his autobiography, Chaplin attempts to analyse the reasons for the intense antagonism he had come to inspire in the United States. 'My prodigious sin', he concludes, 'was, and still is, being a non-conformist.' He was not, he said, a Communist, but he refused to fall in line by hating those who were. He does not hate the American Legion either, despite their offences against him. The Legion, he acknowledges, has achieved many constructive ends. It is only when the legionnaires exceed their legitimate purposes and rights, and under the guise of patriotism encroach upon the freedom of others that 'they commit an offence against the fundamental structure of the American Government. Such super-patriots could be the cells to turn America into a fascist state'.

His second offence, he said, was his opposition to the Committee on Un-American Activities, a dishonest phrase, he vividly remarked, 'elastic enough to wrap around the throat and strangle the voice of any American citizen whose honest opinion is a minority one'. His third offence was that he never attempted to become an American subject: how many American citizens, he asked, have lived and worked for decades in Britain without taking out British citizenship; 'and the English have never bothered about it.'

The stay in England was eventful enough. The original object of their coming had been the première of *Limelight*. It was a première in the old, grand manner, attended by Princess Margaret, fêted by a vast crowd in Leicester Square and filmed for television (the first and only time for a Chaplin première). Later there was the hob-nobbing with the great which had characterized Chaplin's previous European visits. Chaplin was increasingly concerned with world events ('At this juncture', he says in his book, 'I think it appropriate to sum up the state of the world as I see it today') and particularly with nuclear disarmament. He was disappointed to find Herbert Morrison, as a socialist, in favour of atomic defence; less surprised when Lord Salisbury clearly disapproved of his own stance, which was to be expressed in *A King in New York*.

In France and Italy sympathy with the exile was even more apparent. In Paris Chaplin was invested with the rank of Officer of the Légion d'Honneur. The *Limelight* première was a brilliant affair; and the Chaplins were guests of honour at a special performance by the Comédie Française. They dined with Picasso, Sartre and Aragon – to the horror of Chaplin's publicity man, Harry Crocker, who felt that such a meeting would effect the final wreck of Chaplin's reputation in the United States, and who was not consoled by Chaplin's joke that Stalin would be joining them later. Afterwards Picasso took them to his studio, 'a deplorable, barnlike garret, that even Chatterton would have been loth to die in'. In Rome their reception was somewhat marred by a demonstration by young neo-fascists at the première of *Limelight*; but Chaplin professed himself amused to be the target for vegetables, and refused to press charges against a few who were arrested.

Limelight *1952. Calvero, the tragic clown, removes his make-up.*

After many months of a hotel existence, the Chaplins reluctantly recognized Switzerland as financially the best sanctuary for exiles like themselves, and settled in an early nineteenth century mansion in thirty-seven acres, at Corsier sur Vevey. Here Chaplin was to spend the twenty-three years of life that remained to him, marvelling at the total happiness of his last marriage, and coping with the problems of bringing up a large, young family. The house at Vevey became a place of pilgrimage for Chaplin's friends and admirers; and the meetings with the great ones of the world continued. Chaplin's autobiography relates, with pleasant pride, his encounters with Khruschev, Nehru, Chou-en-lai and Churchill, who rebuked him when they met at the Savoy for not replying to a letter of congratulation after *Limelight*, two years before.

The years of exile were by no means a period of retirement. While living

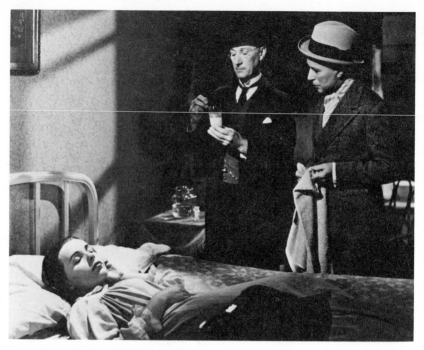

Limelight *1952. Chaplin as Calvero, with Wheeler Dryden and Claire Bloom.*

in Switzerland Chaplin had two more films, *A King in New York* and *A Countess from Hong Kong* to make; and to the end of his life he continued work on *The Freak*, which was intended to star his daughter Victoria.

Chaplin's creative urge was unquenchable. In 1964 he wrote that he was in good health and still creative, and had plans to produce more pictures – 'perhaps not with myself, but to write and direct them for members of my family'. He was, he said, 'still very ambitious; I could never retire. There are many things I want to do; besides having a few unfinished cinema scripts, I should also like to write a play and an opera – if time will allow'. One of the illustrations in the book is a watercolour by Chaplin himself of Oona, which captures a rather vivid likeness.

Lillian Ross, the *New Yorker* writer, contributed to the magazine a lively recollection of her intermittent friendship with the Chaplins. The article later appeared in the form of a slim volume as *Moments With Chaplin*. Among her memories is seeing Chaplin at work on *My Autobiography*, which was to be published when he was seventy-six:

'Charlie Chaplin, at five o'clock in the morning, heading quietly for his study, to work alone on his autobiography, as he did every morning for several years. In 1962, on an afternoon in early September, I sat with him on his terrace as he read parts of his book manuscript to me, the tortoise-shell rimmed glasses a bit down on his nose, his reading dramatic to the point of melodrama, his devotion to his subject unselfconscious and complete.'

Chaplin told her during a pause in his recital, 'I do all my own editing. I'm very particular. I like to see a clean page, with no erasures. I'm completely self-taught.'

*　　*　　*

There was a footnote, too, to the 1964 autobiography. In 1974 The Bodley Head, which had published *My Autobiography*, published Chaplin's last book, *My Life in Pictures*. It was a handsome album, with pictures from Chaplin's own collections, many of them never reproduced before.

The commentary, in the first person, was mostly a summary of the larger autobiography; but Chaplin added a few notes to bring his story up to date. 'In May 1971 I was made a Commander of the Legion of Honour at the Cannes Film Festival. And in October the following year I returned to Holly-

Michael Chaplin, Charles Chaplin, Oliver Johnston.

wood to receive a special Academy Award. I was touched by the gesture – but there was a certain irony about it somehow.'

Francis Wyndham provided an introduction to this new book, which included a sensitive description of Chaplin's life with his fourth wife and their family: with this marriage, history, instead of repeating itself in a boringly predictable way, 'now went into a spectacular reverse. It turned out that Oona's inner nature was of a piece with her outward beauty. She is clever, witty, calm, loyal and totally lacking in self-regard or self-interest. She has made her love for him the centre of her own life, with the result that he soon came to depend on her entirely. Their marriage is perfectly happy. When she comes, rather shyly, into the room, he reaches out a hand to hold hers; he will interrupt any conversation to blurt out, unembarrassingly, how much he adores her ... If she leaves his side for a moment, he looks distressed until her return. Himself a sensitive, proud, egotistic, touchy man, the essential artist, he marvels at those qualities which make her the ideal artist's wife: tolerance, intuition, tact. The only flaw in their domestic harmony – occasional misunderstandings with their children as each in turn ceases to be a child – springs from the very intensity and completeness of their mutual happiness. The delight which Charlie and Oona take in each other's company tends to isolate them in a self-sufficient world of love'.

Wyndham also in this essay summarized, perhaps better that any other writer has done, the essential and mythical element in Chaplin's work: 'There is a contradiction at the heart of Chaplin's work, which has always been excitingly ahead of its time while simultaneously expressing a reassuringly old-fashioned quality. Although his great celebrity was achieved as early as 1914 in the most "modern" of all art forms, the cinema, his performances were essentially the perpetuation of an ancient tradition. Through his apprenticeship in the music-halls (which were themselves then well past their prime) he was able to develop a pantomimic gift which had its origins in the strolling tumblers of the Middle Ages and the classic sophistication of the Commedia dell'Arte, emerging as master of a comedy technique both simple and refined, where the crudest farce can be interpreted with the purest style.

'This accounts for the extraordinary, almost subliminal power of those first flickering appearances, which seized on the world's imagination through means other than words and has never quite relinquished it. Charles Chaplin is more than just famous; his image remains part of our psychic heritage. For members of several generations, it literally recalls their childhood – but its hold goes deeper than that. It seems to belong to some universal, almost abstract concept of childhood, beyond time and space; like certain passages in Dickens, it is as familiar and mysterious as a recurring dream.'

Opinion of the Fifties

As he had in each of the two preceding decades, Chaplin made two films in the fifties. *Limelight* was his last American film; *A King in New York*, made at the age of 68, his first British picture.

When Theodore Huff published his 1951 biography, he was able to report that for the past two years Chaplin had been working on a script to be called *Footlights*, thereby scotching rumours that he was about to retire.

Limelight, as the film was eventually called, was completed in the Autumn of 1952. Chaplin's first draft script is said to have run to some 700 pages. The work was clearly very close to his experience and his heart, with a strong element of spiritual and actual autobiography about it. Chaplin's own current situation had evident parallels with the story of the old star whose public had deserted him; and in the love that springs between this man and a young girl. At the same time the setting of the film was the world he had known in his own youth, the world of the London music hall just before the First World War. The character of Calvero, the old clown who has hit failure, hard times and the bottle, was in part based, said Chaplin, on the American comedian Frank Tinney whom he had seen on stage in the days of his stardom and then years later when his self-confidence had deserted him. There was also no doubt some memory of Marceline, the famous clown who starred at the London Hippodrome when the infant Chaplin was playing a cat in pantomime, and whom he also saw in later years when his nerve and stardom had gone; and there was certainly something of Chaplin's own father, who had fallen victim to that occupational hazard of performers in the Victorian and Edwardian music halls, the bottle. No doubt, too, there was some memory of his mother in the little ballet girl who has lost the will to dance and to live.

Chaplin recreated the London of his memory in his studio, very far away from the reality, in California. Yet *Limelight* is the most English of his films. His recreation of London was, as James Agee had written of Monsieur Verdoux's Paris, 'a highly intelligent paraphrase'. The film opens with Chaplin, as the clown Calvero, weaving unsteadily back to his lodgings in a house that looks very like those in the terraces of Kennington. He is watched curiously by three bright-eyed urchins who were in fact his own children,

Geraldine, Michael and Josephine.

Inside the house he is rapidly sobered up by the discovery of the unconscious girl, Terry (Claire Bloom), who has attempted to commit suicide by gassing herself. Despite the disapproval of their landlady (the fine veteran character actress Marjorie Bennett) Calvero takes her to his own rooms to care for her. He discovers that a psychosomatic illness has convinced her that she is unable to dance or even to walk. Over the weeks, as he works to bring new hope and life to her, he begins to experience some return of his own old optimism; and Terry persuades him to attempt a come-back. His first attempts are discouraging.

Terry is however nursed back to health, and her confidence in her own ability is so far restored that she becomes a star of the Empire Ballet. Calvero is given a comedy role in the ballet, but is sacked as being not funny enough. Already understanding that Terry's romantic devotion to him is standing in the way of her true love for a young composer, Calvero walks out of her life.

He is only rediscovered much later by the young composer (played by Sydney Chaplin), who by this time has joined up: it is 1914 and the First

Limelight *1952. Chaplin as Calvero with Claire Bloom.*

Limelight *1953. Chaplin with Claire Bloom.*

World War has begun. The composer and Terry persuade Calvero to accept the offer of a benefit performance in which he will star.

The performance that follows is one of the cinema's most touching homages to the past, and to the age of pantomime. Calvero's partner in his stage act is played by Buster Keaton – it was the only time the two greatest comedians of the silent cinema had ever appeared together. Keaton, groping behind huge pebble-glasses, accompanies Chaplin's performance on a violin. The act begins with a series of dreadful misadventures: Chaplin's legs keep changing length beneath his huge clown-trousers; Keaton is overwhelmed by an avalanche of sheet music; they are both involved in the disintegration of the piano; and Keaton succeeds in standing on Calvero's violin. Eventually, with a new violin pulled out of the back of his trousers, Calvero manages to continue with his performance. It ends in a climax of slapstick, with Calvero falling off the stage into the bass drum.

The finale of the film is sentiment as unrestrained as any Victorian melodrama, yet somehow wholly authorized by the authenticity of the film's period character. Chaplin is unable to get out of the drum: he has been struck by a heart attack. He is carried on to take his bow, makes a brave farewell, still in the drum. He urges Terry to go on stage and perform her ballet. He dies proudly watching her dancing.

A King in New York *1957. Chaplin as King Shahdov. Appearing in a commercial for liquor, he has unwisely sampled the product he is promoting.*

Six years later it was a very different Chaplin who re-emerged in the role of *A King in New York*. This was the most angry and bitter film Chaplin ever made – and indeed one of the most ferocious feature films any artist has ever created out of his own experience. The underlying strength of Chaplin's humour and sentiment, both alike unquenchable, still triumphs over the resentments of the moment. The triumphs, it must be admitted, are comparative. Chaplin himself frankly confessed that this was his least successful film. The Chaplin studio could provide those 'intelligent paraphrases' for London or Paris; but London locations were an unconvincing impersonation of New York.

So many of Chaplin's targets too were ugly, unlovely and unlovable – sex films, noise pollution, cosmetic surgery, television commercials – that the results were often ugly too. The English supporting players with their variously unconvincing American accents added to a general air of shabbiness. In retrospect however the defects apply mostly to the incidentals of the film. The central story – the King's relation with the small boy, played by Michael Chaplin, whose parents are victims of the Un-American Activities persecution

A King in New York *1957. Chaplin, unable to make himself heard above the din of the orchestra, signifies in mime to the waiter that he desires turtle soup. Oliver Johnston on left.*

– has about it something of the feeling of *The Kid*, with Jackie Coogan's economic deprivations supplanted, in Rupert's case, by a much worse kind of spiritual betrayal.

It was inevitable that Chaplin should wish to make a satire on his sufferings in America as a form of exorcism. Graham Greene, in an open letter to Chaplin published in *The New Statesman and Nation* shortly after Chaplin's removal into exile, said that he had proposed to Chaplin that he should bring back the old Charlie to the screen, with a very simple plot: Charlie, living forgotten in a New York attic, is suddenly summoned before the House Un-American Activities Committee to account for his past – that is for his suspicious behaviour in the ring in *Modern Times* and other films, and for all the hidden significance of the dance with the bread rolls. The United States Attorney General, suggested Greene, had offered a comic climax as good as anyone could hope for.

Chaplin may also have got some ideas from his encounters with the exiled European royalties who were his neighbours in Switzerland. His auto-biography recalls meetings in the early fifties, for instance, with the Queen of Spain.

Chaplin plays King Shahdov, who arrives off the plane in New York, after being dethroned by a revolution in his kingdom of Estrovia. His object in coming to New York is to use a fortune banked there for peaceful developments of atomic energy. Unfortunately he discovers that the money has all been spirited away by his crooked Prime Minister.

Shahdov encounters some of the hazards of contemporary American society, among them rock and roll, CinemaScope and television commercials. Invited to a party, he is tricked into a candid camera television appearance. The public reaction is so favourable however as to persuade him to eke out the diminished treasury by appearing in commercials arranged by a personable young woman (Dawn Addams) who has attracted his amorous interest.

It is in the course of a visit to a progressive school that he meets little Rupert McAbee whose aggressive political lectures elicit from Shahdov the opinion that he is 'Obnoxious, offensive, but a genius'. Later he again meets the boy, who has run away from school because Government agents want to question him about the political affiliations of his parents. Rupert's father is cited for contempt of Congress when he refuses to name names; Rupert himself is taken into custody; and the King, because of his connexion with the child, is called before the Un-American Activities Committee. Despite some confusion with a hose-pipe which results in the Committee being drenched, the King is cleared of Communist associations. He decides to shake the dust of America from his feet; but before leaving visits Rupert in school. He finds the boy spiritually broken, shamed and sobbing at having 'named names' in order to free his parents.

*   *   *

Chaplin found the press 'luke-warm' over *Limelight*. In fact, while the American reviews were in large part coloured by Chaplin's personal unpopularity, the English newspapers had something of a field-day of nostalgia. The Chaplin family figured much in the press at the time of the *Limelight* opening; and if London did not turn out to mob Chaplin quite as it had done thirty years before, the British were distinctly protective to its returning son and to his tribute to the England of his youth.

Understandably, *A King in New York* was not exhibited in the United States in 1957, though the American newspapers published reports of British and European reaction to the film. *Time* was characteristic of the hostile tone of most writers: 'Convinced that he had been persecuted by McCarthyism, head-liner Chaplin decided to deprive the US of one of the few authentic geniuses produced by the movies. Last week a new Chaplin film, *A King in New York*, which may never be shown in the US had its world première in London.' The crowd, the report said, was enthusiastic about Chaplin but less so for his film. It quoted the *Manchester Guardian*: 'To watch a new Chaplin film without once being made helpless with laughter and without shedding a solitary tear – here is food for tears.' 'Intended as satire' continued *Time*, '*King*'s few funny spots are outweighed by shrill invective and heavy-footed propaganda ... *A King in New York* impressed most critics as being less a labor of love than one of hate. To counteract this general impression, Chaplin told a Foreign Press Association luncheon in London: "I love America even now ... I made the film for laughter". Unfortunately, Chaplin seems to have forgotten that the most unhumorous thing a humorist can do is lose his sense of humour.'

Time, in fact, rather inaccurately sensed the tone of the British press, whose loyalty to Chaplin had evidently not only survived, but had been strengthened by the spectacle of his American misfortunes. There were some qualifications, inevitably: in *The Daily Mail* Cecil Wilson said, 'In comic dumb show Chaplin still has no equal, but serious words render him so inarticulate that I came away yesterday cursing the invention of talkies.' But the rest, almost to a man, though acknowledging defects, were unanimous and unstinting in admiration. The trade press was as usual succinct: 'The master's touch, although erratic, lifts the picture well clear of the ordinary' (*Kine Weekly*); 'That Chaplin magic as joyous as ever in an entertainment compounded of gags, wit, humour, a touch of romance and a hint of tragedy. It can't fail to be an outstanding box-office success with all kinds of audiences' (*Cinema*).

In *The Daily Herald* Margaret Hinxman admitted, 'it is not by any means his funniest, but the least of Chaplin is comparable with the best of almost anybody else. His is genius.' Paul Dehn, a poet and scriptwriter as well as a critic, wrote in *The News Chronicle*: 'Like all the great Chaplin pictures, most of this one is either very funny or very touching. It excites our hatred of what is hatable through our laughter and our tears – mostly, in the present instance, through our laughter. Any American who finds its satire of the transatlantic scene offensive is the wrong sort of American. For what he finds offensive in New York can be just as offensive in London, Paris, Rome or Berlin ... The Little Tramp has sat in judgment on the modern world and played what I trust will not be his Last Trump.'

By chance two of the London newspapers that week chose guest critics both peculiarly representative of their times. John Osborne, then the brightest new star in the British theatre firmament, as the author of *Look Back in Anger*, reviewed the film for *The Evening Standard*: 'Mr Chaplin is one of those rare people who can occasionally seem to be mildly hysterical without losing an ounce of dignity. He can be sentimental and create an emotional reality at the same time. His concern for the world is so bright, so deep is the heart of his genius that even the most startling revelations of his hatred can be turned to sweetness by a simple gesture or a resigned turn of the eyes.

'In some ways *A King in New York* must be his most bitter film. It is certainly the most openly personal. It is a calculated, passionate rage clenched uncomfortably into the kindness of an astonishing comic personality. Like the king in his film, he has shaken the dust of the United States from his

A King in New York *1957. Chaplin, as King Shahdov, is uneasy at the result of cosmetic plastic surgery.*

feet, and now he has turned round to kick it carefully and deliberately in their faces. Some of it is well aimed – some is not.

'In fact, for such a big, easy target, a great deal of it goes fairly wide. What makes the spectacle of misused energy continually interesting is once again the technique of a unique comic actor.'

The guest film critic in *The Observer* was Kenneth Tynan, standing in for the veteran Caroline A. Lejeune. Tynan frankly disliked the film, and yet, 'The curious thing ... is that it is never boring. It is seldom funny, sometimes hysterical and almost always predictable; but it is never boring. Some of it is wildly self-indulgent, as when the writer-director-composer-star recites the words of "To be or not to be" for no perceptible purpose, and gets it wrong into the bargain. Many of the slapstick interludes are both ill-judged and perfunctory; and none of the backgrounds conveys the remotest feeling of America. When it aspires to epigram, the dialogue falls into a quaint, soggy prissiness; when it attempts real feeling, we find ourselves in the dread company of lines like: "To part is to die a little".

'Yet, I repeat, at the risk of boring you: it is never boring. How can this be? Is it Chaplin's genius that sustains our interest? Hardly; for except in fugitive snatches the film shows little evidence of genius at work. The central

A King in New York *1957. King Shahdov mistakes an autograph hunter for a writ server.*

idea – a deposed king finding freedom less free than he had supposed – is full of ironic possibilities; yet there are few sequences on which a script-writer of moderate skill could not have improved. And this, I think is the point: that no one has tried to improve them. Nobody has peered over the author's shoulder, warning him that this line may not go over in Huddersfield or that that situation may give offence in Scranton. Nobody has subjected the script to "a polishing job" which is the film industry's euphemism for the process whereby rough edges are planed away and sharp teeth blunted.

'The result, in the fullest sense of the phrase, is "free cinema", in which anything, within the limits of censorship can happen. In every shot Chaplin speaks his mind. It is not a very subtle mind; but his naked outspokenness is something rare, if not unique in the English-speaking cinema. A crude free film is preferable, any day, to a smoothly fettered one.'

When, finally, in 1976 the film was shown in the United States, such qualities did not seem to reach the critics. *Time* was still the hardest: Richard Schickel wrote that the film 'is regarded in some critical quarters as perhaps the worst movie ever made by a distinguished film maker. Its release in the U.S. for the first time provides no reason to dispute that judgment, although one might nominate Chaplin's most recent picture, *The* (sic) *Coun-*

tess From Hong Kong as an alternate selection . . .'

Andrew Sarris in *The Village Voice* was a good deal more enigmatic. After a review that seemed unequivocally to damn the film's content and manner, he quite suddenly concluded: 'I seem to be developing excuses for not liking it. Actually I love the film.'

*   *   *

A remarkable proliferation of books about Chaplin in the fifties was evidently a direct reaction to the concerted attacks he had suffered in the United States, as admirers and supporters leapt to his defence in print. In England in 1951 the film maker and writer Peter Cotes collaborated with Thelma Niklaus on *The Little Fellow*. It is an adoring biography and a passionate defence: 'He and Dickens are of the same stock, filled with the same humanism, the same passionate pity for the underdog, the same blaze of anger against persecution, exploitation and injustice.' Georges Sadoul, the French Marxist film historian and former adherent of the surrealists, also admired Chaplin's embracing humanism and social idealism, in his 1951 *Vie de Charlot*, which was to be reissued in a number of guises over the succeeding three decades. Meanwhile a newer and highly influential critic, André Bazin, was publishing passionate and closely argued critiques in defence of *Verdoux* and *Limelight*.

Theodore Huff's monumental biography, *Charlie Chaplin*, which was published in the United States also in 1951, stands, with all its faults (and they are few enough) and adulation (genuine enough) as a milestone in Chaplin studies. Huff had compiled the first comprehensive Chaplin filmography six years before. The filmography has been amplified since then; a few more sources have come to light; but by and large, after thirty years, Huff's book still stands as the most sympathetic and substantial account of the career. Huff shared the veneration of most of his comtemporaries of the thirties: 'Chaplin is more than an "actor"; he is a clown, in direct line of descent from the Commedia dell'arte; he is the twentieth-century counterpart of Arlequin and Grimaldi. Thanks partly to the universal nature of the film medium, he has made more people laugh than any other man who ever lived. And beyond this he is a symbol of the age, the twentieth-century Everyman.'

The following year brought a new French study, co-authored by the critic Maurice Bessy and Chaplin's old collaborator the writer-director Robert Florey, and most valuable for Florey's sometimes slightly acid recollections of working as assistant director on *Monsieur Verdoux*. In the United States Robert Payne, styled by Sobel and Francis as 'the most elaborately effusive of Chaplin's admirers' published *The Great God Pan*, which another Chaplin chronicler, Timothy J. Lyons, has described as a 'rhapsodic (and inaccurate) review of the adventures of The Tramp through the films'.

In 1954 José-Augusto Franca's *Charlie Chaplin le Self-Made Myth* was published in French in Lisbon. In England R. J. Minney's journalistic bio-

In exile: Chaplin with Anthony Asquith, London. 1952.

graphy, *Chaplin – The Immortal Tramp*, compensated for shortcomings of research by the fact that Minney personally knew Chaplin's brother, Sydney; and it is always evident that here, sometimes for the first time, we are getting Sydney's version of the early life of the Chaplin boys.

In 1955 Chaplin scholarship took another large step forward with the publication of Glauco Viazzi's *Chaplin e la critica* (Bari: Laterza), a staggering bibliography of 1,041 works with an introductory interpretation of the literature, and an anthology of articles from Delluc to Bazin. Viazzi's work provided a basis for the later and still larger guide to references and resources by Timothy J. Lyons.

The industry was international. In France Jean Mitry, a life-long admirer, finally published his *Charlot et la Fabulation Chaplinesque*; in Brazil Francisco Oliveira e Silva wrote *Don Quixote e Carlito*; in the Soviet Union the first Chaplin study since the ill-fated Eisenstein enterprise, Grigori Alexandrovich Avenarius's *Charles Spencer Chaplin*, appeared. The spate of Chaplin appreciations continued into the sixties: and most were inspired by the barely qualified idolatry of critics of the twenties and thirties, though with added outrage at the injustice which America had done to Chaplin. In 1960 another

163

Soviet study appeared, this time by Alexandr V. Kukarkin. In France Barthélemey Amengual contributed an appreciative and highly cerebral introduction to his anthology, *Charles Chaplin* (with the sixties the more formal first name came more generally into use); and the Marxist critic Marcel Martin offered a careful analysis in his own *Charles Chaplin* (1966). In Britain there was Isabel Quigly's perceptive little monograph on *Charlie Chaplin: Early Comedies* and in the United States a documentation by Mark Ricci and Michael Conway, *The Films of Charlie Chaplin*.

As well as Chaplin's own *My Autobiography* (the superfluous possessive has continued to baffle), members of the Chaplin clan offered their impressions and recollections. The books of Charles Chaplin Jr (1960) and Michael Chaplin (1966) have already discussed. In 1966 too Lita Gray, the second Mrs Chaplin, told her side of the story of *My Life With Chaplin*.

Last Works

All who came into contact with Chaplin understood that he had an irresistible creative drive that was not to leave him to the very end of his life. In 1966, when he was 77 years old, he embarked on a new film: it was to be his last. His courage was astounding. For the first time he worked with colour, with CinemaScope, with major international stars. As in *A Woman of Paris* he himself made only a fleeting, token appearance – this time as a ship's steward suffering from *mal de mer*, a disorder which had provided him with comedy for more than half a century.

Chaplin admitted to a sense of nostalgia in approaching the film. He had considered the story thirty years before, as a vehicle for Paulette Goddard. In the year of *The Dirty Dozen*, *Who's Afraid of Virginia Woolf*, *The Graduate*, *Belle de Jour*, *Weekend* and *Bonnie and Clyde*, a romantic comedy of this type was a brazen anachronism.

Chaplin even began his film with a sub-title: 'As a result of two world wars, Hong Kong was crowded with refugees'. Perhaps the most surprising anachronism was to find among these (after *two* world wars?) an exiled Russian countess, played by Sophia Loren. The Countess, Natascha, working as a dance escort, encounters an American diplomat. When he sets sail for home and an important new post, he finds Natascha stowed away in his cabin. The action of the film is mostly taken up with efforts to conceal the stowaway, her 'marriage' to the diplomat's effete secretary, and the inevitable progress through tiffs and irritation to eventual true love.

Chaplin undoubtedly enjoyed being back on a film set – even if, for the first time, he was not his own producer – but the production was not without difficulties. Marlon Brando, the 'Method' actor *par excellence*, was gravely disconcerted by Chaplin's life-long habit of demonstrating precisely how every line or gesture should be done; and later gave out some hostile press interviews about his director. Loren's veneration and application compensated somewhat. In the course of the filming Chaplin was badly shaken by breaking his ankle.

A fellow-comedian commented interestingly on the difficulties Chaplin faced in the production: in *The Total Film-Maker* Jerry Lewis noted: 'Chaplin saw actors as people, then as dramatic tools. They performed for

Chaplin with Sophia Loren at the London press conference to announce A Countess from Hong Kong *1965.*

him that way. He made the statement that Marlon Brando's casting in *Countess From Hong Kong* was because of Brando's lack of humour. It implies that Chaplin believed he would have comic control over Brando if he played the straight man. His lack of ability as a comedian was an asset. There were scenes when Brando moved like a puppet. The picture went haywire, but Chaplin's planning was correct.

'*Countess From Hong Kong*, which should have had gentler treatment from the critics, went haywire because of time. Just after seeing it I watched a documentary of Jesse Owens, the champion runner. There were shots of him running in the Berlin Olympic Games of 1936 and shots of him walking in 1968. His walk from just one spot to another was frightening. He'd atrophied.

'The same thing happened to Charlie Chaplin. He made *Modern Times* in 1936 and *Countess* in 1967. He hadn't been given the opportunity to stay alive creatively because of the leftist issue. Thirty-one years after *Modern Times* Chaplin was tackling the same problems in a wholly different world with a different speed, different people – different juices. There was no way for his creative mind to cook.'

The years between have achieved an odd compensatory effect. Lewis was quite right that in its time it was a startling anachronism. Seen today, however, no longer linked to a particular period, just a work from an undefined past, it has acquired a gentle, surprising charm; and revivals on television have made the reviews of the time, which at their kindest took a more-in-sorrow-than-in anger line, seem much overstated.

They were, indeed, the cruellest notices Chaplin had ever received; and though he brushed them aside with a bravely truculent declaration to the press that the critics were 'bloody idiots', he was unquestionably hurt by them. *Time* said: '*A Countess From Hong Kong* is probably the best movie ever made by a 77-year-old man. Unhappily it is the worst ever made by Charlie Chaplin ... A substandard shipboard farce that Chaplin wrote, directed and briefly appears in.' In London the *Evening Standard* critic Alexander Walker, always Chaplin's most appreciative critic, reckoned it 'a sad and bitter disappointment'. Chaplin, he wrote, 'has always been at his most brilliant when he doesn't depend on words. Here they let him down in scene after scene'. His own genius at mime, the critic continued, had simply not rubbed off on his new stars.

The Times was thoughtful: 'It is always difficult to separate in one's mind the various functions of a great composite; how much of the effect of a classic Chaplin film is due to his direction, how much to his writing, and how much to his own central performance? The suspicion has always persisted, unconfirmable while *A Woman of Paris*, the only film he directed but did not star in, remained unseeable, that he might be at best a director of very modest competence who just happened to have a rare knack of showing off his own work as a performer to maximum advantage – in contrast to Buster Keaton, for instance, whose film *The General* is one of the most beautifully made films ever.

'Now that Mr Chaplin has again ventured on a film denied the special support of his own performance in a central role, we can take stock. And, sadly, it must be said that *A Countess From Hong Kong* confirms our most pessimistic imaginings. The story was first conceived around 1940, and it is interesting to speculate on how differently the film should affect us if it had been made then with Chaplin himself and Paulette Goddard playing the roles now played by Marlon Brando and Sophia Loren. But speculation is vain: the film was not made until now, and as it stands it is likely to be a saddening experience for all lovers of Chaplin's earlier work.

'Chaplin's comedy has always depended mainly on human observation, on the funniness of human beings as they really are and really react. But here neither of the principal characters is for a moment believable, and the humour comes not from real possibilities of their situations but from their incessantly being compelled to act in a way no one would act, to say things no one would say, just in order to raise a quick laugh.'

The Times reviewer and a sentence in the *Time* article – '*Countess* is bad enough to make a new generation of moviegoers wonder what the Chaplin cult was all about' – set the tone of a good deal of criticism in this last phase of Chaplin's working life. In Britain particularly there was an evident reaction to the adulation of earlier generations, a compulsion to iconoclasm. 'I never really find Chaplin funny' became a constant rebuke, taken by the writer or speaker to be in itself sufficiently damning, and leaving out of account the billions of ordinary viewers who across more than half a century and the whole world *had* found Chaplin funny, the funniest man in the world. One of the bases of late sixties and seventies criticism was adverse comparison with Buster Keaton – already indicated by the *Times* critic. The comparison, failing to acknowledge what a limitless field the creation of comedy can be, produced debates as arid as attempts to relate Dickens and Thackeray or Tennyson and Donne.

Some reaction against the lyrical enthusiasm of Chaplin's admirers at the prime of his creation (In the twenties Alexander Woollcott's lachrymose eulogia became notorious) was of course inevitable. Inevitably, too, it tended mostly to be recorded in periodical literature rather than book-form studies of Chaplin. People who write books generally do so because they are in love with their subject. One of the most articulate and vitriolic dismissals of Chaplin did, however, appear in volume form, in the Bio-

A Countess from Hong Kong *1966. Chaplin on set with Margaret Rutherford and Sophia Loren.*

graphical Dictionary of the Cinema (Secker & Warburg, 1975) composed by an entertainingly waspish English critic, David Thomson.

Having traced to psychological injuries suffered in his youth such adult traits as his 'delirious egotism', his 'overbearingly winsome personality', mawkishness, coy charm and heartless cold pathos always focused on himself, sentimentality, over-refinement, cruelty that is 'also feminine, impetuous and instinctive', hostility to the world, his sympathy-grabbing, Thomson credits Chaplin with intuitively sensing how ready the viewer was to have his fantasies indulged.

'But that instinct has usually lacked artistic intelligence, real human sympathy and even humour. Chaplin's isolation has barred him from working with anyone else. He needs to fulfil every creative function on a film, whether it is scripting, composing or directing actors. He is isolated, too, in the sense that his later films seem as cut off from any known period or reality as the earlier ones. That eery feeling one has in reading the later parts of *My Autobiography*, that Chaplin is still unable to appreciate the world on any other than his own terms, is borne out by the films which supposedly deal with the world's problems but in a social setting that seems increasingly implausible ...

'His later films are dreadful ... The early work seems to me narrow when put beside the films of Keaton and the Marx Brothers. But the early shorts do have a strange sophistication that derives from Chaplin's intuitive skill at easing himself into an audience's mind ...' (Chaplin's most hostile critics of the period generally felt on safe ground in praising the 'prentice works, before the Chaplin persona was clearly formed).

'His political philosophy was actually threadbare and the move now looks like a final retreat into the cloud cuckoo land of Switzerland ... In truth, Chaplin is the looming mad politician of the century, the demon tramp. It is a character based on the belief that there are "little people". Whereas art should insist that people are all the same size.'

A more temperate view of the need to revalue Chaplin in relation to his contemporaries in Hollywood silent comedy was that of Donald W. McCaffrey, published in 1968, seven years before Thomson's *Dictionary*: 'It is easy to become rhapsodic after being captured by the charm of this comedian. Chaplin's works are emotionally charged and provoke such responses. As an antiquarian in love with silent screen comedy, I am naturally enthusiastic myself. I believe however, he has been overrated at the expense of his contemporaries, Harold Lloyd, Buster Keaton and Harry Langdon. I find much in Chaplin that makes him the greatest clown of our age, but not the Everyman, or the Sir Galahad. There is a profundity in the tramp – a dimension that places him on a high plane; yet I believe that many critics attribute qualities to him that go beyond the province of the clown. Granted, many of these comments make interesting reading (and may give their author the label of a penetrating critic with intellectual insights that soar above the commonplace. After all, why write about that which is easily detected?), but such views are often limited, impressionistic, and too individualistic, even though they may promote appreciation for the art they applaud. On the other hand, the drama of the comedian is usually underrated or even dismissed as something entertaining and consequently of little significance. Therefore, I take a qualified stand. The clown may touch upon the profundities of life, but this is an added dimension. Primarily, this little fellow who is dancing in the wind, thumbing his nose, or embracing the good things of life, is concerned with the pleasure of laughter which he promotes. He is, in short, an entertainer, a bearer of happiness. It is not necessary to excuse him, to apologize for him, to elevate him. As if making us laugh were of little significance.' McCaffrey's comments appeared in a book on *Four Great Comedians* – Chaplin, Lloyd, Keaton, Langdon. His undoubted admiration for Chaplin was to be expressed two years later when he published a valuable anthology of writings on Chaplin, *Focus on Chaplin*.

The older evaluation of Chaplin would still find expression in books like *A Discovery of Cinema*, by the veteran film maker, Thorold Dickinson: 'none could surpass his pathos and the implications of social comment that enriches his work'. Gerald Mast, an American academic (who was once a child actor) could still boldly affirm in 1973: 'Charles Chaplin is the greatest film artist in motion-picture history. He is to the movies what Shakespeare is to the drama. And, like Shakespeare, he is so because he has both something interesting inside his head and the technical skill to take what is inside him and turn it into something objective and visible that is powerful, stimulating, haunting and moving. Whereas Shakespeare's tools were dramatic structure and the English language, Chaplin's were his hypnotic performances themselves and his cinematic ability to capture and communicate these performances'. (*The Comic Mind.*)

Endeavouring to reconcile the conflict, another American writer Robert Sklar, in his *Movie-Made America – A Cultural History of American Movies* (1975) wrote: 'In recent years, reacting against the effusive adulation Chaplin received, some critics have insisted he was only one of many exceptional silent comedians, and that he borrowed techniques and ideas from others as well as they from him. Undoubtedly this is true. Yet it misses the essential Chaplin, the inimitable Chaplin – the man who made comedy and pathos out of working-class people's lives and dreams.'

Much more interesting, however, was the work of those few critics who genuinely offered revaluation rather than devaluation. Easily the most appreciative, perceptive and original assessment of Chaplin's work is that of an uneven but dazzlingly creative critic, Raymond Durgnat, in *The Crazy Mirror: Hollywood Comedy and the American Image*. He concludes, after a convincing defence of *Modern Times*:

'To over-idealize Chaplin into an inoffensive Little Man, all pathos and lovable mischief, a sort of Saint Chaplin, is not only to miss half of his humour and meaning, it is to make nonsense of all that really can be called

Chaplin at work on A Countess from Hong Kong *1966.*

Chaplin's comedy of the misplaced soul. To be misplaced it has to be perched in someone who's incongruous and unworthy, who's infra dig, who has a guttersnipe's reflexes and lack of scruple. The mainspring of Chaplin's genius is, in a sense, the spiritual vividness which he gives to the basic, undignified physical things, fleas, feet, sausages. His one semi-failure, *A King in New York*, is also the one film that cut loose from these basics and lost itself in generalizations about society. Deep thinkers are two a penny nowadays; but guttersnipes like Charlie are worth their weight in gold'.

The last years of Chaplin's life, when his performing days were over, saw a still greater proliferation of monographs. In France there was a new book by an old admirer, Pierre Leprohon's *Charlie Chaplin*, and Maurice Bessy and Robin Livio's biography of the same, plain title. In Germany there was Joe Hembus's *Charlie Chaplin und Seine Filme*. There was a spate of detailed critical documentations of Chaplin's *oeuvre*, in Italy, Francesco Savio's *Il Tutto Chaplin*, in France Jean Mitry's *Tout Chaplin*, in Sweden Uno Asplund's *Chaplin i Sverige* which was translated into English as *Chaplin's Films*.

The final years of Chaplin's life saw four new biographies in English. Denis Gifford's *Chaplin* in a series called *The Movie Makers* (London, Macmillan, 1974) was new and stimulating for an essentially show-business flavour which placed the Chaplin of Karno and Keystone firmly in their historical perspective. Robert Manvell's *Chaplin*, contributed to Hutchinson's Library of World Biography (1975) with a succinct and comprehensive account, which managed to retain an historical perspective upon Chaplin's career and reputation:

'Charlie Chaplin possessed undoubted genius during the prolonged period of his creativity, stretching from his embryonic work in 1914 at least to the period of *Limelight* in 1952. This already exceeds the span of Dickens's major works from the time of *Pickwick Papers* (1836) to the unfinished novel *Edwin Drood* (1870). While it would be unrealistic to compare the work of these two very different artists of the highest order who worked in very different media, it would not perhaps be unfair to say that Chaplin has occupied much the same place in the hearts of the people of the twentieth century that Dickens occupied in the nineteenth, and that, because he was working in a new and internationalized visual medium, his public during the height of his success has been incomparably larger in numbers. If there is any creative artist with whom Charlie might care to be classed, it is probably Dickens. It seems to me right to do so'. A third English publication, whose title *Sir Charlie* acknowledged the knighthood accorded to Chaplin in the 1975 honours list, was by an American, Edwin P. Hoyt, evidently inspired by deep affection for his subject and shame at the ignobility of America's treatment.

Mention has already been made of *Chaplin, Genesis of a Clown* by Raoul Sobel and David Francis. Elegant, erudite, well researched, the book traced Chaplin's artistic origins in pantomime, *commedia*, the music halls and the

Chaplin in the late sixties.

poverty of Victorian London, offering an elaborate analytical appraisal of his comedy techniques. What gave the book its special piquancy was the recognition (and at what point was the recognition the authors'?) that neither Francis, Curator of the National Film Archive, nor Sobel, a Chaplin devotee, actually *liked* either the man or his work.

A pleasant footnote to Sobel and Francis's discussion of the links between Chaplin and the *commedia dell'arte* came with David Madden's attractive and eccentric little book *Harlequin's Stick – Charlie's Cane* which used images and words to discover parallels between the types and techniques of the *commedia* and silent slapstick movie comedy.

Finale

A Countess From Hong Kong was to be Chaplin's final film, though he never stopped working. For some years he occupied himself with his script for *The Freak*, which would have starred his daughter Victoria; but Victoria married and established a circus with her husband; and it became evident that Chaplin's physical strength would not again be equal to his creative will. He occupied himself putting musical scores on to his old silent films. Barely a year before his death he completed the score for his master-work *A Woman of Paris* which he eventually, reluctantly, reissued, more than half a century after the first disappointment of its rejection by the public of 1923.

At four o'clock in the morning of Christmas Day 1977, Chaplin died at his home in Corsier sur Vevey, Vaud, Switzerland.

His death was the main headline in every newspaper across the world. He was to make headlines some weeks later when – an event which would have tickled his taste for the macabre – his body was stolen from its grave and held for ransom by a couple of out-of-work refugees of Keystone in-competence. There was no equivocation among the obituarists: everyone knew that, with all his faults, the man who had died was the greatest clown of all.

The Times headed its obituary not 'Sir Charles Chaplin', but simply 'Charlie Chaplin': 'He was the last survivor from among the founding fathers of the American cinema, one of the greatest comic creators in films, and achieved greater, more widespread fame in his own lifetime than perhaps anyone else in the history of mankind. He was the darling of the intellectuals, who loved to theorize on the significance of his comedy, its social responsibility, its relation to the great traditions of the commedia dell'arte and circus clowning, its anarchic force and vigour. But he also had to a unique degree the common touch – people of virtually any culture were able to respond with laughter to his screen antics, and for generation after generation of children he was the first introduction to the magic world of the cinema.

'During the latter part of his long life, Chaplin, though loaded with honours and universally regarded as one of the unshakeable monuments of the cinema (whatever controversy his political attitudes might arouse), did begin to suffer from a certain reaction to the excesses of his early admirers. This had something to do with a grudging but progressive disenchantment with his later films, and something to do with the rediscovery and revaluation of the work of his many rivals in silent comedy. As we moved into the 1950s it became permissible to prefer the refined and unsentimental art of Buster Keaton who was certainly a far more subtle and imaginative film-maker than Chaplin could ever claim to be, or even the totally unpretentious humour of Laurel and Hardy. The time was coming, in fact, for a thorough reassessment of Chaplin's own work, concentrating on aspects of it which would be more congenial to modern sensibilities: the elements of childlike ruthlessness which had endeared it to the surrealists, perhaps, rather than the sentimentalizing elevation of the "little man" which had made him a hero to liberal humanism.

'As with Chaplin's performances', this rather grudging acknowledgement of his greatness continued, 'so with his career as a whole, the secret of his success lay in his immaculate timing.'

*   *   *

In the brief time since Chaplin's death a sudden upsurge of interest appears to focus more upon the persona than the work. At the time of writing, several personal biographies, two stage musicals and a film are in preparation; while Lita Gray, the second Mrs Chaplin, promises a new version of her recollections of her celebrated, if temporary husband.

Against this, however, the posthumous period has seen two major contributions to Chaplin scholarship. One is Timothy J. Lyons' astonishing catalogue of Chaplin References and Resources (Boston, G. K. Hall, 1979) which lists, with perceptive commentary, some fifteen hundred literary and other sources.

In 1978 John McCabe, an American professor who had already written classic biographies of Laurel and Hardy and George M. Cohan, published his *Charlie Chaplin*, which for the moment stands as the best account of Chaplin's private, public and creative life. Modestly, McCabe said that his task, as he saw it was simply 'to update and amplify Huff in view of recent scholarship'. His book introduces the additional bonus of rare glimpses of Chaplin in interviews with one of his earliest co-workers in comedy, Stan Laurel.

Another rare and hitherto unknown portrait of Chaplin emerged from Alistair Cooke's *Six Men*, one of the essays in which recalled a brief period in the early thirties when the young Cooke worked with Chaplin and even did some writing on the comedian's legendary Napoleon project. But the most poignant part of his recollections is from a time much later, when the aged and fragile Chaplin went to Hollywood to receive his

Oscar. He was, says Cooke, 'very old and trembly and groping through the thickening fog of memory for a few simple sentences ... he was now – as the song says – "easy to love", absolutely safe to adore'.

The Times obituary now stands as the nadir of ingratitude for a creation that had in its time reached the whole world, and touched so many billions with laughter and pleasure. The balance of opinion was already being redressed, handsomely. Walter Kerr's outstanding analysis of Chaplin's silent films and his artistic developments in *The Silent Clowns* had appeared shortly before Chaplin's death, in 1975. Kerr is at his most perceptive in his study of Chaplin's eventual development of the Tramp out of the variegated hodge-podge of parts he played in the first Sennett films, often related only by the costume. Chaplin's problem, as well as his gift, wrote Kerr, was his ability to be anyone. 'The secret is a devastating one. For the man who can, with the flick of a finger or the blink of an eyelid, instantly transform himself into absolutely anyone is a man who must, in his heart, remain no one. To be able to play a role, to know the role as a role, is to see through it. To be able to play them all is to see through them all. But that leaves nothing, no way of life, no permanent commitment in which such a man can possibly believe ...

'The tramp is a philosophical, not a social, statement. And it was a conclusion to which Chaplin came, not a choice he imposed from the outset. The tramp is the residue of all the bricklayers and householders and *bon vivants* and women and fiddlers and floorwalkers and drunks and ministers Chaplin had played so well, too well. The tramp was all that was left. Sometimes the dark pain filling Chaplin's eyes is in excess of the situation at hand. It comes from the hopeless limitation of having no limitations ...

'The discovery that he could not be anyone because he could be everyone unleashed a number of things in Chaplin. To begin with, it resolved the problem posed by *The Tramp*. He no longer had to alternate between comedy and pathos, developing each one separately. He could be funny and sad at the same time, now that the news about himself was clear'.

Andrew Sarris's magisterial summation of Chaplin's career and art was published shortly after Chaplin's death, in *Cinema: A Critical Dictionary*, edited by Richard Roud. 'Chaplin is arguably the single most important artist produced by the cinema, certainly its most extraordinary performer and probably still its most universal icon ... blessed with total mimetic recall, he was able to communicate emotionally with the troubled masses through all the convulsions of War, Revolution, Inflation, Depression and Disillusion that passed blindly across his pantomimic path. That he treated the symptoms of these convulsions instead of analysing their causes seemed to bother him more than it did his admirers, but the gnawing intellectual insecurity of the artist may ultimately have expanded the informal dimensions of his films and enriched their emotional tone. Thus, it would seem that time is more on the side of his features than of his shorts, and that the most lasting image of Chaplin will be lyrical rather than exuberant, poignant rather

Modern Times, *1936*.

than frenetic. And that the focus of his soul will shift from his floppy feet to his fierce eyes'.

From this it follows that Sarris reacts against the romantic view that the silent era represents the true Chaplin and that all that came after is decline. He attributes equal weight in his evaluation to the last features. Sarris's earlier reviews of the film had revealed his own equivocal feelings about *A King in New York*: here he calls it 'his most misunderstood film, with America as a fantasy and a delusion, a marvellous world which he eventually revisited in triumph, but which he never reconquered'.

Speaking of the last work in general, Sarris concludes, '. . . having survived for so long, Chaplin seemed a study less in decline than in modal metamorphosis, and if his audiences diminished, they gained in appreciation as they contemplated an artist who for more than half a century had used the screen as his personal diary. As he had outgrown Sennett, he had outlasted Hitler, and he had aged with extraordinary grace. He had even got around to recording his awareness (in *Limelight*) that he had lost his mass audience. He remains the supreme exemplification of the axiom that lives and not lenses stand at the centre of cinematic creation'.

Filmography

Credits for the films of Chaplin's early career, made for the Keystone and Essanay companies and for release by Mutual and First National, are presented in tabular form – apparently the first time the method has been adopted to record the films of any director.

This presentation is useful in revealing the stock company system prevailing in these early films and, in the case of the Keystone year, Chaplin's own progress to artistic autonomy. Incidentally it also offers at-a-glance filmographies for the collaborators – directors, writers and actors – in Chaplin's early work.

The numerical system applied in Uno Asplund's filmography *Chaplin's Films* (David and Charles, 1971) has been adopted to avoid the confusion which could result from the existence of two series of numbers.

1914: THE KEYSTONE FILMS

Production: Keystone
Producer: Mack Sennett
Photography: Frank D. Williams (except *Making a Living*, generally credited to E. J. Vallejo)

	Title	Release date	Length	CHARLES CHAPLIN	HENRY LEHRMAN	MACK SENNETT	GEORGE NICHOLS	MABEL NORMAND	JOSEPH MADDERN	CHARLES AVERY	CHARLES CHAPLIN	REED HEUSTIS	HENRY LEHRMAN
				Director							*Scenario*		
1	MAKING A LIVING	February 2	1030		*								*
2	KID AUTO RACES AT VENICE	February 7	572		*								*
3	MABEL'S STRANGE PREDICAMENT	February 9	1016		*	*							*
4	BETWEEN SHOWERS	February 28	1020		*								*
5	A FILM JOHNNIE	March 2	1020				*						
6	TANGO TANGLES	March 9	734		*								
7	HIS FAVOURITE PASTIME	March 16	1009				*						
8	CRUEL, CRUEL LOVE	March 26	1035				*						
9	THE STAR BOARDER	April 4	1020				*						
10	MABEL AT THE WHEEL	April 18	1900					*	*				
11	TWENTY MINUTES OF LOVE	April 20	1009							*	*		
12	CAUGHT IN A CABARET	April 27	2053	*				*			*		
13	CAUGHT IN THE RAIN	May 4	1015	*							*		
14	A BUSY DAY	May 7	441	*							*		
15	THE FATAL MALLET	June 1	1120			*							
16	HER FRIEND THE BANDIT	June 4	1000	*				*					
17	THE KNOCKOUT	June 11	1960						*				
18	MABEL'S BUSY DAY	June 13	998	*				*					
19	MABEL'S MARRIED LIFE	June 20	1015	*				*					
20	LAUGHING GAS	July 9	1020	*							*		
21	THE PROPERTY MAN	August 1	2118	*							*		
22	THE FACE ON THE BAR ROOM FLOOR	August 10	1020	*							*(1)		
23	RECREATION	August 18	462	*							*		
24	THE MASQUERADER	August 27	1030	*							*		
25	HIS NEW PROFESSION	August 31	1015	*							*		
26	THE ROUNDERS	September 7	1010	*							*		
27	THE NEW JANITOR	September 24	1020	*							*		
28	THOSE LOVE PANGS	October 10	1010	*									
29	DOUGH AND DYNAMITE	October 26	2000	*		*					*		
30	GENTLEMEN OF NERVE	October 29	1030	*							*		
31	HIS MUSICAL CAREER	November 7	1025	*							*		
32	HIS TRYSTING PLACE	November 9	2000	*							*		
33	TILLIE'S PUNCTURED ROMANCE	November 14	6000			*							
34	GETTING ACQUAINTED	December 5	1025	*							*		
35	HIS PREHISTORIC PAST	December 7	2000	*							*		

(1) after the poem by Hugh Antoine D'Arcy
(2) from the play, 'Tillie's Nightmare' by Edgar Smith

VIRGINIA RAPPE
HENRY LEHRMAN
ALICE DAVENPORT
CHESTER CONKLIN
MINTA DURFEE
FRANK D. WILLIAMS
GORDON GRIFFITH
PAUL (BILLY) JACOBS
CHARLOTTE FITZPATRICK
THELMA SALTER
HARRY McCOY
HANK MANN
AL ST JOHN
FORD STERLING
EMMA CLIFTON
SADIE LAMPE
ROSCOE ARBUCKLE
MACK SENNETT
PEGGY PEARCE
EDGAR KENNEDY
LEO WHITE
WILLIAM SEITER
JOSEPH SWICKARD
PHYLLIS ALLEN
ALICE HOWELL
WALLACE MACDONALD
MACK SWAIN
CHARLES MURRAY
GEORGE SUMMERVILLE
CHARLES PARROTT (CHARLEY CHASE)
JOE BORDEAUX
EDWARD CLINE
BILLIE BENNETT
FRITZ SCHADE
EDWARD SUTHERLAND
CHARLES BENNETT
LEE MORRIS
CECILE ARNOLD
VIVIAN EDWARDS
RHEA MITCHELL
JACK DILLON
NORMA NICHOLS
MARIE DRESSLER
G. G. LIGON
REV D. SIMPSON
GENE MARSH

1915–1916: THE ESSANAY FILMS

Production: Essanay
Producer: Jess Robins
Director: Charles Chaplin
Scenario: Charles Chaplin
Photography: Roland Totheroh, Harry Ensign (except *His New Job* and *Police*, which are credited to Totheroh alone)
Assistant director: Ernest Van Pelt (except *His New Job*)
Scenic Artist: E. T. Mazy (credited from *Work* onwards)

Title	Release date	Length ft	CHARLES CHAPLIN	EDNA PURVIANCE	BEN TURPIN	CHARLOTTE MINEAU	CHARLES INSLEY	LEO WHITE	FRANK J. COLEMAN	GLORIA SWANSON	AGNES AYRES	BUD JAMISON	FRED GOODWINS	BILLY ARMSTRONG	PADDY MCGUIRE	CARL STOCKDALE	LLOYD BACON	G. M. ANDERSON	MARGIE REIGER	ERNEST VAN PELT	MARTA GOLDEN	JOHN RAND	WESLEY RUGGLES	LAWRENCE A. BOWES	JAMES T. KELLEY	DEE LAMPTON	MAY WHITE	CARRIE CLARKE WARD	JACK HENDERSON	PHYLLIS ALLEN
36 HIS NEW JOB	February 1st	1896	*		*	*		*		*	*	*																		
37 A NIGHT OUT	February 15	1856	*	*	*			*				*	*																	
38 THE CHAMPION	March 11	1938	*	*				*				*		*	*	*	*	*		*										
39 IN THE PARK	March 18	984	*	*				*				*		*			*		*	*										
40 A JITNEY ELOPEMENT	April 1	1958	*	*				*				*	*		*	*	*													
41 THE TRAMP	April 11	1896	*	*				*					*	*	*		*			*										
42 BY THE SEA	April 29	971	*	*								*		*	*				*											
43 WORK	June 21	2019	*	*			*	*						*	*						*									
44 A WOMAN	July 12	1788	*	*			*							*					*		*									
45 THE BANK	August 16	1985	*	*			*	*	*				*	*	*	*						*	*	*						
46 SHANGHAIED	October 4	1771	*	*				*				*		*								*	*	*						
47 A NIGHT IN THE SHOW	November 2	1735	*	*		*		*				*			*							*	*		*	*	*	*		
48 CHARLIE CHAPLIN'S BURLESQUE ON CARMEN	April 22 1916	3986	*	*				*	*			*										*	*				*		*	
49 POLICE	May 27 1916	2050	*	*				*	*			*	*	*								*	*		*					*

1916–1917: THE MUTUAL FILMS

Production: Lone Star Mutual
Producer: Charles Chaplin
Director: Charles Chaplin
Scenario: Charles Chaplin
Photography: Roland Totheroh and William C. Foster
Scenic Artist: E. T. Mazy (credited on *The Floorwalker, The Fireman, One A.M.*)

Title	Release date	Length	Cast
51 THE FLOORWALKER	*May 15	1734 ft	CHARLES CHAPLIN, EDNA PURVIANCE, ERIC CAMPBELL, ALBERT AUSTIN, LLOYD BACON, LEO WHITE, CHARLOTTE MINEAU, TOM NELSON, JAMES T. KELLEY, FRANK J. COLEMAN, JOHN RAND
52 THE FIREMAN	*June 12	1921	CHARLES CHAPLIN, EDNA PURVIANCE, ERIC CAMPBELL, ALBERT AUSTIN, LLOYD BACON, LEO WHITE, JAMES T. KELLEY, FRANK J. COLEMAN, JOHN RAND
53 THE VAGABOND	*July 10	1956	CHARLES CHAPLIN, EDNA PURVIANCE, ERIC CAMPBELL, ALBERT AUSTIN, LLOYD BACON, LEO WHITE, CHARLOTTE MINEAU, JAMES T. KELLEY, FRANK J. COLEMAN, JOHN RAND, WESLEY RUGGLES
54 ONE A.M.	August 7	2000	CHARLES CHAPLIN, ALBERT AUSTIN
55 THE COUNT	September 4	2000	CHARLES CHAPLIN, EDNA PURVIANCE, ERIC CAMPBELL, ALBERT AUSTIN, JAMES T. KELLEY, FRANK J. COLEMAN, JOHN RAND, PHYLLIS ALLEN, MARTA GOLDEN
56 THE PAWNSHOP	October 2	1940	CHARLES CHAPLIN, EDNA PURVIANCE, ERIC CAMPBELL, ALBERT AUSTIN, HENRY BERGMAN, JAMES T. KELLEY, FRANK J. COLEMAN, JOHN RAND, LOYAL UNDERWOOD
57 BEHIND THE SCREEN	November 13	1796	CHARLES CHAPLIN, EDNA PURVIANCE, ERIC CAMPBELL, ALBERT AUSTIN, LEO WHITE, CHARLOTTE MINEAU, HENRY BERGMAN, JAMES T. KELLEY, FRANK J. COLEMAN, JOHN RAND, EVA THATCHER
58 THE RINK	December 4	1881	CHARLES CHAPLIN, EDNA PURVIANCE, ERIC CAMPBELL, ALBERT AUSTIN, HENRY BERGMAN, JAMES T. KELLEY, FRANK J. COLEMAN, JOHN RAND, LEOTA BRYAN
59 EASY STREET	January 22 1917	1757	CHARLES CHAPLIN, EDNA PURVIANCE, ERIC CAMPBELL, ALBERT AUSTIN, LEO WHITE, CHARLOTTE MINEAU, HENRY BERGMAN, JAMES T. KELLEY, FRANK J. COLEMAN, JOHN RAND, LEOTA BRYAN
60 THE CURE	April 16	1834	CHARLES CHAPLIN, EDNA PURVIANCE, ERIC CAMPBELL, ALBERT AUSTIN, HENRY BERGMAN, JAMES T. KELLEY, STANLEY SANFORD, FRANK J. COLEMAN, JOHN RAND, EVA THATCHER, LOYAL UNDERWOOD, JANET MILLER SULLY, TOM WOOD
61 THE IMMIGRANT	June 17	1809	CHARLES CHAPLIN, EDNA PURVIANCE, ERIC CAMPBELL, ALBERT AUSTIN, HENRY BERGMAN, JAMES T. KELLEY, STANLEY SANFORD, FRANK J. COLEMAN, JOHN RAND, MAY WHITE, EVA THATCHER, LOYAL UNDERWOOD, JANET MILLER SULLY, KITTY BRADBURY
62 THE ADVENTURER	October 22	1845	CHARLES CHAPLIN, EDNA PURVIANCE, ERIC CAMPBELL, ALBERT AUSTIN, HENRY BERGMAN, JAMES T. KELLEY, FRANK J. COLEMAN, JOHN RAND, LOYAL UNDERWOOD, TORAICHI KONO, MONTA BELL

*Story co-credit with Vincent Bryan

185

1918–1923: FIRST NATIONAL FILMS

Production: Chaplin–First National
Producer: Charles Chaplin
Director: Charles Chaplin
Scenario: Charles Chaplin
Photography: Roland Totheroh
Assistant: Charles Riesner

Title	Release date	Length	CHARLES CHAPLIN	EDNA PURVIANCE	SYDNEY CHAPLIN	ALBERT AUSTIN	TOM WILSON	HENRY BERGMAN	JAMES T. KELLEY	CHARLES RIESNER	BILLY WHITE	JANET MILLER SULLY	BUD JAMISON	LOYAL UNDERWOOD	PARK JONES	JACK WILSON	JOHN RAND	TOM WOOD	TOM TERRISS	BABE LONDON	RAYMOND LEE	JACKIE COOGAN	CARL MILLER	PHYLLIS ALLEN	NELLIE BLY BAKER	JACK COOGAN	MONTA BELL	LILLITA GREY	'SCRAPS'	MACK SWAIN	REX STOREY	ALLAN GARCIA	LILLIAN McMURRAY	KITTY BRADBURY	DINKY DEAN RIESNER	MAI WELLS	TOM MURRAY	EDITH BOSTWICK	FLORENCE LATIMER
63 A DOG'S LIFE	1918 March 12	2674 ft	*	*	*	*	*	*	*	*	*	*	*	*	*														*										
64 THE BOND	July 27	685	*	*	*	*	*	*						*																									
65 SHOULDER ARMS	October 4	3142	*	*	*	*	*	*						*		*	*																						
66 SUNNYSIDE	1919 June 4	2769	*	*			*	*						*				*	*																				
67 A DAY'S PLEASURE	November 26	1714	*	*			*	*												*	*	*																	
68 THE KID	1921 January 17	5300	*	*		*	*	*		*												*	*	*	*	*	*	*											
69 THE IDLE CLASS	September 6	1916	*	*				*		*																				*		*							
70 PAY DAY	1922 March 13	1892	*	*																				*						*		*							
71 THE PILGRIM	1923 January 24	4300	*	*				*		*																				*				*	*	*	*	*	*

ESSANAY PERIOD: UNAUTHORIZED FILMS

THE ESSANAY–CHAPLIN REVUE (1916); An anthology of *The Tramp*, *His New Job* and *A Night Out*.

50. TRIPLE TROUBLE (1918): an amalgam, assembled by Leo White, of scenes from *Police*! and an uncompleted Essanay short, *Life*, with new material shot by White.

1923–1952: THE UNITED ARTISTS RELEASES

72

A WOMAN OF PARIS

Production: Regent–United Artists
Producer: Charles Chaplin
Director: Charles Chaplin
Story/Scenario: Charles Chaplin
Photography: Roland Totheroh
Cameraman: Jack Wilson
Assistant director: Edward Sutherland
Literary editor: Monta Bell
Art director: Arthur Stibolt
Research: Jean de Limur, Henri d'Abbadie d'Arrast

Release date: 1st October 1923
Length: 7,577 feet

  CAST:
  Edna Purviance (Marie St Clair)
  Adolphe Menjou (Pierre Revel)
  Carl Miller (Jean Millet)
  Lydia Knott (Jean's Mother)
  Charles French (Jean's Father)
  Clarence Geldert (Marie's Father)
  Betty Morrissey (Fifi)
  Malvina Polo (Paulette)
  Henry Bergman (Head waiter)
  Harry Northrup (Valet)
  Nelly Bly Baker (Masseuse)
  Charles Chaplin (Porter)

73

THE GOLD RUSH

Production: Chaplin–United Artists
Producer: Charles Chaplin
Director: Charles Chaplin
Story/Scenario: Charles Chaplin
Photography: Roland Totheroh

Cameraman: Jack Wilson
Technical director: Charles D. Hall
Assistant directors: Charles Reisner, Henri d'Abbadie d'Arrast
Production manager: Alfred Reeves

Release date: 16th August 1925
Length: 8,555 feet

Reissue version, 1942

Music: Charles Chaplin
Commentary: written and spoken by Charles Chaplin
Length: 8,498 feet

> CAST:
> Charles Chaplin (The Lone Prospector)
> Georgia Hale (Georgia)
> Mack Swain (Big Jim McKay)
> Tom Murray (Black Larsen)
> Betty Morrissey (Georgia's friend)
> Malcolm Waite (Jack Cameron)
> Henry Bergman (Hank Curtis)
> John Rand, Heinie Conklin, Albert Austin, Tom Wood, Allan Garcia (Prospectors)

74

THE CIRCUS

Production: Chaplin–United Artists
Producer: Charles Chaplin
Director: Charles Chaplin
Story/Scenario: Charles Chaplin
Photography: Roland Totheroh
Cameramen: Jack Wilson, Mark Marklatt
Assistant director: Harry Crocker
Art director: Charles D. Hall

Release date: 6th January 1928
Length: 6,500 feet

Reissue version, 1970

Music: Charles Chaplin
Song: Charles Chaplin, sung by himself
Length: 6,400 feet

> CAST:
> Charles Chaplin (Charlie, A Tramp)
> Merna Kennedy (The Equestrienne)
> Betty Morrissey (The Vanishing Lady)
> Allan Garcia (Circus Proprietor)
> Harry Crocker (Rex, King of the High Wire)
> Henry Bergman (Clown)
> Stanley J. Sanford (Head Property Man)

George Davis (Magician)
John Rand (Assistant Property Man)
Steve Murphy (Pickpocket)
Doc Stone (Prizefighter)

75

CITY LIGHTS

Production: Chaplin–United Artists
Producer: Charles Chaplin
Director: Charles Chaplin
Story/script: Charles Chaplin
Photography: Roland Totheroh
Cameramen: Mark Marklatt, Gordon Pollock
Assistant directors: Harry Crocker, Henry Bergman, Albert Austin
Art director: Charles D. Hall
Music: Charles Chaplin
Musical director: Alfred Newman
Music Arranger: Arthur Johnson

Release date: 1st February 1931
Length: 7,815 feet

   CAST:
Charles Chaplin (The Tramp)
Virginia Cherrill (The Blind Girl)
Florence Lee (Her Grandmother)
Harry Myers (Millionaire)
Hank Mann (Boker)
Allan Garcia (Butler)
Henry Bergman (Mayor *and* Janitor)
Albert Austin (Street sweeper *and* Crook)
Robert Parrish (Newsboy)
John Rand (Tramp)
James Donelly (Foreman)
Stanhope Wheatcroft (Man in Cafe)

Jean Harlow and her mother are believed to appear as extras.

76

MODERN TIMES

Production: Chaplin–United Artists
Producer: Charles Chaplin
Director: Charles Chaplin
Story/script: Charles Chaplin
Photography: Roland Totheroh, Ira Morgan
Assistant directors: Carter De Haven, Henry Bergman
Art directors: Charles D. Hall, J. Russell Spencer
Music: Charles Chaplin; Leo Daniderff ('Je Cherche apres Titine')

Musical director: Alfred Newman
Musical Arrangers: Edward Powell, David Raksin

Release date: 5th February 1936
Length: 7,634 feet

CAST:
Charles Chaplin (A Worker)
Paulette Goddard (Gamine)
Henry Bergman (Proprietor)
Stanley J. Sanford (Big Bill)
Chester Conklin (Mechanic)
Hank Mann (Burglar)
Stanley Blystone (Sherriff Coulet)
Allan Garcia (President)
Dick Alexander (Convict)
Cecil Reynolds (Chaplain)
Myra McKinney (Chaplain's Wife)
Lloyd Ingraham (Governor)
Louis Natheaux (Addict)
Heinie Conklin (Workman)
Frank Moran (Convict)

77

THE GREAT DICTATOR

Production: Chaplin–United Artists
Producer: Charles Chaplin
Director: Charles Chaplin
Story/script: Charles Chaplin
Photography: Roland Totheroh and Karl Struss
Editor: Willard Nico
Art director: J. Russell Spencer
Music: Charles Chaplin; Wagner, Brahms
Musical director: Meredith Willson
Sound: Percy Townsend, Glenn Rominger
Assistant directors: Wheeler Dryden, Daniel James, Robert Meltzer
Coordinator: Henry Bergman

Release date: 15th October 1940
Length: 11,319 feet

CAST:
Charles Chaplin (Adenoid Hynkel *and* The Barber)
Paulette Goddard (Hannah)
Jack Oakie (Benzino Napaloni)
Henry Daniell (Garbitsch)
Reginald Gardiner (Schultz)
Billy Gilbert (Herring)
Maurice Moskovich (Mr Jaeckel)

Emma Dunn (Mrs Jaeckel)
Bernard Gorcey (Mr Mann)
Paul Weigel (Mr Agar)
Grace Hayle (Madame Napaloni)
Carter De Haven (Ambassador)
Chester Conklin (Customer in Barber's Shop)
Hank Mann (Stormtrooper)
Eddie Gribbon (Stormtrooper)
Leo White (Barber)
Lucien Prival (Officer)
Richard Alexander (Stormtrooper)
also, Pat Flaherty, Harry Semels, Esther Michelson, Florence Wright, Robert O. David, Eddie Dunn, Peter Lynn Hayes, Nita Pike, Jack Perrin.

78

MONSIEUR VERDOUX

Production: Chaplin–United Artists
Producer: Charles Chaplin
Director: Charles Chaplin
Story/script: Charles Chaplin. *From an idea by:* Orson Welles
Photography: Roland Totheroh, Curt Courant, Wallace Chewing
Editor: Willard Nico
Art director: John Beckman
Music: Charles Chaplin
Musical director: Rudolph Schrager
Sound: James T. Corrigan
Costumes: Drew Tetrick
Associate director: Robert Florey
Assistant directors: Rex Bailey, Wheeler Dryden
Narrator: Charles Chaplin

Release date: 11th April 1947
Length: 10,961 feet

CAST:
Charles Chaplin (Monsieur Henri Verdoux)
Martha Raye (Annabella Bonheur)
Isobel Elsom (Marie Grosnay)
Marilyn Nash (The Girl)
Robert Lewis (Maurice Bottello)
Mady Correll (Mona Verdoux)
Allison Rodell (Peter Verdoux)
Audrey Betz (Martha Bottello)
Ada-May (Annette)
Marjorie Bennett (Maid)
Helen Heigh (Yvonne)
Margaret Hoffman (Lydia Floray)
Irving Bacon (Pierre Couvais)
Edwin Mills (Jean Couvais)

Virginia Brissac (Carlotta Couvais)
Almira Sessions (Lena Couvais)
Eula Morgan (Phoebe Couvais)
Bernard J. Nedell (Prefect)
Charles Evans (Detective Morrou)
Arthur Hohl (Estate Agent)
John Harmon (Joe Darwin)
Vera Marshe (Mrs Darwin)
William Frawley (Jean la Salle)
Fritz Lieber (Priest)
Barbara Slater (Florist)
Fred Karno Jr (Mr Karno)
Barry Norton (Guest)
Pierre Watkin (Official)
Cyril Delevanti (Postman)
Charles Wagenheim (Friend)
Addison Richards (Manager)
James Craven (Friend)
Franklin Farnum (Victim)
Herb Vigran (Reporter)
Boyd Irwin (Official)
Paul Newland (Guest)
Joseph Crehan (Broker)
Wheaton Chambers (Druggist)
Frank Reicher (Doctor)
Wheeler Dryden (Salesman)
also Christine Ell, Lois Conklin, Tom Wilson, Phillips Smalley.

Edna Purviance is erroneously listed as an extra in some Chaplin filmographies.

79

LIMELIGHT

Production: Chaplin–United Artists
Producer: Charles Chaplin
Director: Charles Chaplin
Story/script: Charles Chaplin
Photography: Karl Struss
Photographic consultant: Roland Totheroh
Editor: Joseph Engel
Art director: Eugene Lourie
Music: Charles Chaplin
Songs: Charles Chaplin, Ray Rasch
Choreography: Charles Chaplin, Andre Eglevsky, Melissa Hayden
Associate director: Robert Aldrich
Assistant Producers: Jerome Epstein, Wheeler Dryden

Release date: 23rd October 1952
Length: 12,459 feet

192

CAST:
Charles Chaplin (Calvero)
Claire Bloom (Terry-Tereza)
Nigel Bruce (Mr Postant)
Buster Keaton (Partner)
Sydney Chaplin (Neville)
Norman Lloyd (Bodalink)
Marjorie Bennett (Mrs Alsop)
Wheeler Dryden (Doctor *and* Clown)
Barry Bernard (John Redfern)
Leonard Mudie (Doctor)
Snub Pollard (Musician)
Andre Eglevsky (Harlequin)
Melissa Hayden (Columbine)
Charles Chaplin Jr (Clown)
Geraldine Chaplin (Child)
Michael Chaplin (Child)
Josephine Chaplin (Child)
also Loyal Underwood, Stapleton Kent, Mollie Blessing, Julian Ludwig.

Edna Purviance is erroneously listed as an extra in some Chaplin filmographies.

1957–1966: LATE PRODUCTIONS

80

A KING IN NEW YORK

Production: Attica-Archway
Producer: Charles Chaplin
Director: Charles Chaplin
Story/script: Charles Chaplin
Photography: Georges Perinal
Editor: Jean Seabourne
Art director: Allan Harris
Music: Charles Chaplin
Sound: Spencer Reeves

Release date: 12th September 1957
Length: 9,891 feet

CAST:
Charles Chaplin (King Shahdov)
Dawn Addams (Ann Kay)
Oliver Johnson (Jaumé)
Maxine Audley (Queen Irene)
Jerry Desmonde (Prime Minister)
Michael Chaplin (Rupert McAbee)
Harry Green (Lawyer Green)
Phil Brown (Headmaster)
John McLaren (Mr McAbee)
Allan Gifford (School Superintendent)

Shani Wallis (Singer)
Joy Nichols (Singer)
Joan Ingram (Mona Cromwell)
Sidney James (Johnson)
Robert Arden (Lift Boy)
Nicholas Tannar (Butler)
Lauri Lupino Lane (Comedian)
George Truzzi (Comedian)
also George Woodbridge, Macdonald Parke

81

A COUNTESS FROM HONG KONG

Production: Universal
Producer: Jerome Epstein
Director: Charles Chaplin
Story/script: Charles Chaplin
Photography: Arthur Ibbetson
Editor: Gordon Hales
Production designer: Don Ashton
Art director: Robert Cartwright
Set decorator: Vernon Dixon
Music: Charles Chaplin
Musical director: Lambert Williamson
Musical associate: Eric James
Sound: Michael Hopkins
Sound recording: Bill Daniels, Ken Barker
Assistant director: Jack Causey
Production supervisor: Denis Johnson
Titles: Gordon Shadrick
Colour: Technicolor. CinemaScope

Release date: 2nd January 1967
Length: 11,033 feet

CAST:
Marlon Brando (Ogden Mears)
Sophia Loren (Countess Natascha Alexandroff)
Sydney Chaplin (Harvey Crothers)
Tippi Hedren (Martha Mears)
Patrick Cargill (Hudson)
Margaret Rutherford (Miss Gaulswallow)
Michael Medwin (John Felix)
Oliver Johnston (Clark)
John Paul (Captain)
Angela Scoular (Society Girl)
Peter Bartlett (Steard)
Bill Nagy (Crawford)
Dilys Laye (Saleswoman)
Angela Pringle (Baroness)

Jenny Bridge (Countess)
Arthur Gross (Immigration Officer)
Balbina (Maid)
Anthony Chin (Hawaiian)
Geraldine Chaplin (Girl at Dance)
Jose Sukhum Boonlve (Hawaiian)
Janine Hill (Girl at Dance)
Burnell Tucker (Receptionist)
Leonard Trolley (Purser)
Len Lowe (Electrician)
Francis Dux (Head Waiter)
Cecil Cheng (Taxi Driver)
Ronald Rubin (Sailor)
Michael Spice (Sailor)
Ray Marlowe (Sailor)
Josephine Chaplin (Young Girl)
Victoria Chaplin (Young Girl)
Kevin Manser (Photographer)
Marianne Stone (Reporter)
Lew Luton (Reporter)
Larry Cross (Reporter)
Bill Edwards (Reporter)
Drew Russell (Reporter)
John Sterland (Reporter)
Paul Carson (Reporter)
Paul Tamarin (Reporter)
Carol Cleveland (Nurse)
Charles Chaplin (An Old Steward)

Bibliography/Acknowledgments

The Publishers and Author are grateful for permission for quotations from the following publications:

Adeler, Edwin & West,Con: *Remember Fred Karno* (Long, 1939)

Agee, James: *Agee on Film* (N.Y. McDowell-Oblensky, 1958)

Arnheim, Rudolf (in *Films*, 1946)

Bakshy, Alexander: Review of *The Circus* (in *The Nation*, 1928)

Barnes, Howard: Review of *Monsieur Verdoux* (in *Herald Tribune*, 1946)

Bowman, William Dodgson: *Charlie Chaplin: His Life and Art* (George Routledge, 1931)

Cahn, William: *Harold Lloyd's World of Comedy* (George Allen and Unwin, 1966)

Chaplin, Charles: *My Autobiography* (Bodley Head, 1964)

Chaplin, Charles: *My Life in Pictures* (Bodley Head, 1974)

Chaplin, Charles: *My Wonderful Visit* (Hurst and Blackett, 1922)

Chaplin, Charles, Jr: *My Father, Charles Chaplin* (Longmans, Green and Company, 1960)

Chaplin, Michael: *I Couldn't Smoke Grass on My Father's Lawn ...* (Leslie Frewin, 1966)

Chaplin, Sydney: 'Father Makes a Film' (in *Everybody's*, 1952)

Cooke, Alistair (ed.): *Garbo and the Night Watchmen* (Cape, 1937; rep. Secker and Warburg, 1971)

Cooke, Alistair: *Six Men* (The Bodley Head, 1977)

Cotes, Peter, and Niklaus, Thelma: *The Little Fellow* (Paul Elek, 1951)

Delluc, Louis: *Charlot* (Maurice de Brunhoff, 1921)

Dickinson, Thorold: *A Discovery of Cinema* (O.U.P., 1971)

Exceptional Photoplays (National Board of Review)

Ferguson, Otis: Review of *Modern Times* (in *Garbo and the Night Watchmen*)

Fergusson, Francis: Review of *City Lights* (in *The Bookman*, 1931)

Francis, David and Sobel, Raoul: *Chaplin: Genesis of a Clown* (Quartet Books, 1977)

Goodman, Paul: 'Chaplin Again, Again and Again' (in *Partisan Review*, November–December 1940)

Gordon, Jan and Cora: *Stardust in Hollywood* (Harrap, 1930)

Hackett, Francis: 'The Kid' (in *New Republic*, 20 March 1921)

Harrison, Louis Reeves: 'His Trysting Place' (in *The Moving Picture World*, October 1914)

Head, June: *Stargazing* (Peter Davies, 1931)

Huff, Theodore: *Charlie Chaplin* (Schuman, 1951)

Howe, Herbert: 'What's the Matter with Chaplin?' (in *Picture-Play*, December 1920)

Kaufman, Stanley (ed): *American Film Criticism*, (Liveright, 1972)

Lewis, Jerry: *The Total Film-Maker* (Vision Press, 1971)

McCabe, Jack: *Charlie Chaplin* (Robson Books, 1978)

McCaffrey, Donald W.: *Four Great Comedians* (Zwemmer/Barnes, 1968)

Manvell, Roger: *Chaplin* (Hutchinson, 1975)

Minney, R. J.: *Chaplin, The Immortal Tramp* (Newnes, 1954)

New Masses (reviews by Robert Forsythe and Harry Alan Potamkin)

O'Higgins, Harvey: 'Chaplin' (in *New Republic*, 3rd February 1917)

Osborne, John: Review of *A King in New York* (in *The Evening Standard*, 12th September 1957)

Ross, Lillian: *Moments With Chaplin* (Dodd, Mead & Co., 1980)

Sarris, Andrew: *'Chaplin'*, in Roud, Richard (ed): *A Critical Dictionary of the Cinema* (*Secker and Warburg, 1980*)

Scotland, John: *The Talkies* (Crosby, Lockwood, 1954)

Seldes, Gilbert: *The Great Audience* (Viking Press, 1950)

Sennett, Mack, and Shipp, Cameron: *King of Comedy* (Doubleday, 1954)

Thomson, David: *A Biographical Dictionary of the Cinema* (Secker and Warburg, 1973 rep. 1980)

Time Magazine

Times, The

Tyler, Parker: *Chaplin, Last of the Clowns* (Vanguard Press, 1948)

Tynan, Kenneth: Review of *A King in New York* (in *The Observer*, 15th September 1957)

Wahl, Lucien, Florey, Robert: *Charlie Chaplin* (Paris: Pascal, 1927)

Walker, Alexander: Review of *A Countess From Hong Kong* (in *The Evening Standard*, November 1966)

Wilson, Edmund: Review of *The Gold Rush* (in *The New Republic*, November 1925)

Young, Stark: Review of *The Circus* (in *The New Republic*, 8th February 1928)

Index